Microsoft Lync 2013 Unified Communications: From Telephony to Real-time Communication in the Digital Age

Complete coverage of all topics for a unified communications strategy

Daniel Jonathan Valik

BIRMINGHAM - MUMBAI

Microsoft Lync 2013 Unified Communications: From Telephony to Real-time Communication in the Digital Age

First published: April 2013

Production Reference: 1170413

Published by Packt Publishing Ltd.
Livery Place
35 Livery Street
Birmingham B3 2PB, UK.

ISBN 978-1-84968-506-1

www.packtpub.com

Cover Image by Mark Holland (m.j.g.holland@bham.ac.uk)

Credits

Author
Daniel Jonathan Valik

Reviewers
Gianluca Bellu

Desmond LEE

Joanna Lee

Acquisition Editor
Mary Nadar

Lead Technical Editor
Azharuddin Sheikh

Technical Editors
Worrell Lewis

Sharvari Baet

Project Coordinator
Shraddha Vora

Proofreaders
Aaron Nash

Lesley Harrison

Indexer
Tejal R. Soni

Graphics
Aditi Gajjar

Abhinash Sahu

Production Coordinator
Arvindkumar Gupta

Cover Work
Arvindkumar Gupta

About the Author

Daniel Jonathan Valik is an industry expert in Unified Communications & Collaboration, Cloud, Mobile Platform, Social Networking, and Contact Center technology. He drives the above topics for more than 15 years in the IT and Telecommunication industry and has also lived and worked in different regions like Europe, South East Asia, and United States.

He is a Sr. Program Manager - Unified Communications in the Global Business Operations & Strategic Services division at the Microsoft Headquarters in Redmond/WA, USA and he drives the evolution and maintenance of the global Customer Support Unified Communications strategy. This includes gathering, consolidating and prioritizing business requirements from international customers, business partners and Microsoft business teams to push Microsoft Lync, Lync online, Skype and other unified communications related technology in the field of customer care and global contact centers. In other words, He is responsible for driving innovation in Contact Centers and is working to bring the customer care of Microsoft into the next century of communication and collaboration.

He was born and grew up in "Baden bei Wien" in Austria and started his early career at a small computer shop in his hometown close to Vienna, Austria where he worked as a hardware engineer on PCs and servers. After his first job, he served in the Military for about a year and continued his career as a Systems Engineer for Linux Debian and Suse support at a small telecommunications provider. Then he moved on to a well-known service and software company in Germany, Materna Information and Communications, where he designed, developed and led customer projects for Unified Messaging, Speech Recognition and mobile technology projects in Western Europe.

After almost 6 years in Materna as Systems Engineer, Architect, Presales expert and later as the Product Solution Manager, he made his move to Microsoft Austria and Western Europe. In this new opportunity, he was a Senior Product Specialist for unified communications and Mobility and was responsible for developing and executing 'go to market' initiatives to help enterprises evaluate and justify investment for adoption of Microsoft UC technologies/solutions. During this time he developed partnerships with Samsung, HTC, Polycom, HP, Kapsch, Telekom Austria, T-Mobile, T-Systems, Bechtle, Dialogic, AudioCodes and many other international companies. He also played the role of Project Architect to integrate Microsoft Unified Communications & Collaboration (UCC) solutions with third party equipment and devices like Nortel IP PBX with Exchange's Unified Messaging, Polycom HDX 9000 conferencing system with Microsoft OCS R2, Dialogic gateway with OCS, and so on. As the lead of UCC @ Cloud initiative, he led the team to help customer evaluate options (On-premise, cloud base or hybrid) and develop business cases enabling customer's executives to make informed decisions. Next to this, he also led the initiative to help customers evaluate UCC technologies/solutions (especially OCS/Lync versus Cisco and IBM) by providing solution scenarios, technology comparisons, competitive analysis and Communication-Enabled Business Process (CEBP) to make a 'facts' based decision with ROI justification and alignment of business and IT objectives. This process often required him to play the Architect role to design, build and execute Proof of Concept (POC) projects to support the Microsoft product marketing and product management teams.

After Microsoft Austria, he made another career decision to move his home base to Hong Kong and then Singapore where he drove business development, product management and product marketing for unified communications for an important Microsoft Lync partner, Unify Square APAC.

He holds a number of technical certifications including MCT (Microsoft Certified Trainer). He has a double Master's Degree (MBA) and a Master Degree (MAS) in General Business, additionally he hold a degree for International Business Management. He is the author of several books like "The Renaissance of Communication and Collaboration" (http://www.microsoft.com/uc/de/at/default.aspx), which was the first German book about UC with a mix of business and technology, published as the Lync Server 2010 launch book for the DACH region by Microsoft. Together with Jochen Kunert (Managing Director of Unify Square EMEA), he co-authored the second book about unified communications (http://de.netlog.com/go/out/url=http%3A%2F%2Fwww.microsoft-press.de%2Fproduct.asp%3Fcnt%3Dproduct%26amp%3Bid%3Dms-5222%26amp%3Bapid%3D60091). His third book is about Cloud Services (Migration to the Cloud http://www.amazon.de/s/ref=nb_sb_noss_1?__mk_de_DE=%C5M%C5Z%D5%D1&url=search-alias%3Daps&field-keywords=tobias+h%F6llwarth) which was written for the EuroCloud association in Europe. Additionally he has a couple of other publishing projects, including of whitepapers for Microsoft, Gartner, Formicary Collaboration Group, and others.

He is a regular speaker at international events and congresses like EuroCloud Congress Western Europe, Microsoft Lync Conferences (Lync 2013 Conference San Diego, USA), Microsoft Global Exchange US, TechEd, Microsoft Product Launches, University and campus events and also contributes to technical articles, business magazines and newsletters in Microsoft & Lync forums. In his free time, he spends time with Aikido, Iaido, Kendo, Ken-Jutsu, Kyudo, meditation, Bonsai breeding & aquariums, traveling, reading, snowboarding, running, cooking, music, canopy and hiking.

I would like to thank everyone who supported me during this book project, especially my family and friends. Special thanks to Joanna Lee, who supported me in this book project.

About the Reviewers

Gianluca Bellu has started his IT career in 2001 in Rome (Italy) as systems engineer focused on Microsoft infrastructures and developer for Line of Business applications at Nextiraone Italy, a System Integrator company 15 countries.

In 2004, he was an IVR developer on Alcatel technologies and call center engineer. From 2006, he started to work on Microsoft Office Communications Server 2007 (since it was in beta version) and he was responsible for business proposal and pre/post-sales activities based on Microsoft UC as a new and innovative technology.

Gianluca is now Microsoft Certified IT Professional (MCITP) on Lync Server and Microsoft Certified Application Developer (MCAD); during his career he also achieved Cisco CCNA certification, Snom certification (SCE), and other certifications from Audiocodes, Cycos, and Genesys.

He runs a blog at `http://msucblog.wordpress.com` where he shares his know-how on Microsoft unified communications.

Desmond LEE specializes in end-to-end enterprise infrastructure solutions built around proven business processes and people integration across various industries backed by over a decade of global field experience.

He is recognized as a Microsoft Most Valuable Professional (MVP Lync Server) for his passion and volunteer work in the IT community. He is a long-time Microsoft Certified Trainer (MCT) and founder of the Swiss IT Pro User Group (`www.swissitpro.com`), an independent, non-profit organization for IT Pros by IT Pros championing Microsoft technologies.

An established speaker at major international and regional events known for his real-world insights, he contributes frequently to several highly rated publications and engages as a moderator in popular Microsoft public forums/newsgroups. You can follow his IT adventures at `www.leedesmond.com`.

Joanna Lee loves technology. As she reviewed this upcoming unified communications book, she has also learnt a lot about this particular topic as well. Other than reviewing books, she also does game development. She has programmed for an action game, KengoZero on the Xbox360 and for a Massively Multiplayer Online Games (MMOG), Otherland, on the PC. She is a game designer and has a collection of game design/writings. Her interest in the mobile/web has led her to develop apps and games for these popular platforms as well. Do keep a look out for her apps/games when they are launched! Just a note, she is not just a tech mouse, she also loves food, travelling, taking photos and spending time with family and friends.

I would like to thank my family and friends for letting me take time away from them to review this book.

www.PacktPub.com

Support files, eBooks, discount offers and more

You might want to visit www.PacktPub.com for support files and downloads related to your book.

Did you know that Packt offers eBook versions of every book published, with PDF and ePub files available? You can upgrade to the eBook version at www.PacktPub.com and as a print book customer, you are entitled to a discount on the eBook copy. Get in touch with us at service@packtpub.com for more details.

At www.PacktPub.com, you can also read a collection of free technical articles, sign up for a range of free newsletters and receive exclusive discounts and offers on Packt books and eBooks.

http://PacktLib.PacktPub.com

Do you need instant solutions to your IT questions? PacktLib is Packt's online digital book library. Here, you can access, read and search across Packt's entire library of books.

Why Subscribe?

- Fully searchable across every book published by Packt
- Copy and paste, print and bookmark content
- On demand and accessible via web browser

Free Access for Packt account holders

If you have an account with Packt at www.PacktPub.com, you can use this to access PacktLib today and view nine entirely free books. Simply use your login credentials for immediate access.

Instant Updates on New Packt Books

Get notified! Find out when new books are published by following @PacktEnterprise on Twitter, or the *Packt Enterprise* Facebook page.

Table of Contents

Preface

This book is all about real-time communication and collaboration—in other words all that you need to know about unified communications!

The book combines both interesting areas; business, and technology, into one single literature. The reader will get to know all important key areas of unified communications technologies: How to evaluate and integrate unified communications project in your own company or for your customer, how you select the right solution, how you plan, design, and implement the technology itself, and also how you can create a compelling business case for communications and collaborations projects. Additionally, you get to know the current innovations and available technologies for social networking, collaboration, cloud services, contact centers and enhanced collaboration for mobile devices. This book also offers a real business case of a transformational project from traditional telecommunications to unified communications technology including all key lessons, best practices and how to put together a business case you can use for your business. On the technical side: Let's get to know Microsoft Lync 2013, what's new in one of the most successful unified communications products and what innovative changes we would have in the way we communicate and collaborate in the next few years!

What this book covers

Chapter 1, Innovation of the Communication and Information Technology, introduces you to the current changes in the communication and information technology and the trends that we will see in the next few years. From the beginning of telecommunication, to the Internet and today: unified communications, collaborations, social networking, and cloud technology.

Chapter 2, Information Technology Meets Knowledge Management, explains how collaboration and communication and social networking technology can help businesses to learn faster, store "knowledge" as content, share information across the boundaries of the organization and how communication technology can create better success. Learn about the term Knowledge Management means and how important it is for companies in today's business.

Chapter 3, Business Cooperation in the World of the World Wide Web, explains how unified communications can help companies to be more efficient and more successful. You will also learn how cooperation, partnerships, and alliances between companies are key factors in today's business. To work with another company in partnership also requires a modern communication and collaboration interface.

Chapter 4, Value and Potential for End Users, illustrates a "common business day" with all the modern tools so that you are better connected to customers, business partner, friends, family and be always up-to-date with the latest information. We discuss how chat, VoIP, video conferencing, desktop, application sharing, Lync, and Skype changed our daily lives. You will also learn more about a daily life with unified communications and collaborations technology.

Chapter 5, Cost Optimization Approaches, drives you through important cost saving factors since every company wants to achieve more with less using the most optimal resources. Factors such as facility, data connection, telecommunication costs, insourcing or outsourcing to cloud services and the "real" Return of Investment (ROI) of unified communications for companies of all sizes are discussed. This chapter provides also a very helpful guideline on how you can develop a business case and ROI for a unified communications project.

Chapter 6, Unified Communications Projects in Practice, brings you through a real project example where unified communications is introduced and implemented successfully. It also answers questions such as; What was the business justification? Was the key problem resolved? Why did the company select unified communications for their business? Learn about all key areas of a real-time communication project that are critical to the successful optimization of a company.

Chapter 7, Analyzing the Key Points of a Unified Communications Project, provides great information on how a unified communications project should be introduced, what preparation is required from business and technology side, how to select the best solution for the business, how a successful project needs to be managed and controlled, and how an overall successful outcome can be made a reality. It also answers questions such as: What are the key challenges for a real time or in other words unified communications and collaborations project? What usually blocks projects in this space and how can you resolve challenges to implement a successful project and technology? Learn more about how to realize a successful project and change for the company.

Chapter 8, Technology Inside the Microsoft UC platform and a Look into the Future, provides detailed technical information on how you plan, design, implement, and run a Microsoft Lync 2013 topology for your organization. Microsoft Lync is one of the most successful unified communications solutions in the Information Technology world. Learn also about other tools such as Skype, add-ons for reporting, business intelligence, Contact Center solutions, web chat, persistent chat and great partner solutions for the Lync platform. This chapter will also provide you with an interesting look into the near future of technology.

Who this book is for

Do you want to know more about unified communications, collaborations, Lync, Skype, social, or cloud services? This book offers interesting content for many different audiences: Business decision makers, technical advocates, and IT decision makers. As this is also a fundamental book on real-time collaboration technology, it is suitable for anyone who is interested in the future of communications and collaborations. You will also learn to plan, design, and realize a project in this space for your own company or customers. Through this book's chapters you will gain an in-depth knowledge of topics such as meeting business requirements with UC, how to build a business case, selecting the best technology, plan for UC business solutions such as contact center and CRM integration, realizing projects to migrate from traditional telephony to unified communications inside an organization, and optimize communication and collaboration for your own business, your business partners or your customers.

Conventions

In this book, you will find a number of styles of text that distinguish between different kinds of information. Here are some examples of these styles, and an explanation of their meaning.

New terms and **important words** are shown in bold. Words that you see on the screen, in menus or dialog boxes for example, appear in the text like this: "The following screenshot shows the page when the **Clients** option is selected."

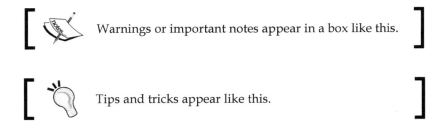

Warnings or important notes appear in a box like this.

Tips and tricks appear like this.

Reader feedback

Feedback from our readers is always welcome. Let us know what you think about this book—what you liked or may have disliked. Reader feedback is important for us to develop titles that you really get the most out of.

To send us general feedback, simply send an e-mail to feedback@packtpub.com, and mention the book title via the subject of your message.

If there is a topic that you have expertise in and you are interested in either writing or contributing to a book, see our author guide on www.packtpub.com/authors.

Customer support

Now that you are the proud owner of a Packt book, we have a number of things to help you to get the most from your purchase.

Errata

Although we have taken every care to ensure the accuracy of our content, mistakes do happen. If you find a mistake in one of our books—maybe a mistake in the text or the graphics—we would be grateful if you would report this to us. By doing so, you can save other readers from frustration and help us improve subsequent versions of this book. If you find any errata, please report them by visiting http://www.packtpub.com/submit-errata, selecting your book, clicking on the **errata submission form** link, and entering the details of your errata. Once your errata are verified, your submission will be accepted and the errata will be uploaded on our website, or added to any list of existing errata, under the Errata section of that title. Any existing errata can be viewed by selecting your title from http://www.packtpub.com/support.

Piracy

Piracy of copyright material on the Internet is an ongoing problem across all media. At Packt, we take the protection of our copyright and licenses very seriously. If you come across any illegal copies of our works, in any form, on the Internet, please provide us with the location address or website name immediately so that we can pursue a remedy.

Please contact us at copyright@packtpub.com with a link to the suspected pirated material.

We appreciate your help in protecting our authors, and our ability to bring you valuable content.

Questions

You can contact us at questions@packtpub.com if you are having a problem with any aspect of the book, and we will do our best to address it.

1

Innovation of Communication and Information Technologies

In this book, we will introduce you to the interesting subjects of communication and collaboration. You will see the present approaches and forms of information processing and what it means to stay connected. We will also look into future technological developments.

Before we delve deep into the technologies, software solutions, and innovative communication capabilities, let me first ask you several questions:

- Have you ever considered how important communication is in your daily life?

- How much do you communicate every day, or how many people do you converse with daily on various issues?

- Is this exchange of information important and necessary?

Communication is not something which we consciously think about in most situations. However, let me urge you to start observing how often you communicate daily with others and particularly the ways and means you do this. I think you can then agree that communication and targeted exchange of information are basic components and a foundation of our lives. Living creatures communicate with one another via some form of tool or other means. In the prehistoric era, humankind communicated information using images, characters, sounds, and later music from the sender to the receiver. However, the uniqueness of this information was not always clearly given and messages communicated by this means did not always reach the intended recipient.

Looking into the past, the origin of cooperation was to create success, whether in career opportunities or social recognition to secure survival for his fellow men and himself.

In the course of time and history, many possibilities derived from technical-evolutionary ideas have been developed for communication, cooperation, and exchange of information over many centuries. Ultimately it is the human drive to be successful and efficient in communicating, processing, and transmitting information that drives this process.

Let us look back at the technological developments that have taken place at the end of the nineteenth century and the beginning of the twentieth century. At that time, our "modern" information exchange and communication by telegraphy (1837, Samuel Morse F. B.) or telephony (1876, Alexander Graham Bell) were in their infant stages. Telephones were innovative pieces of equipment that had to be integrated into companies or offices in order to process information more efficiently and rapidly without having to go through an interconnecting party. These developments were tools of communication which eventually seeded the development of today's modern communication— an integrated solution for communication and collaboration, in short, unified communications/unified messaging.

Defining communication

A communication tool is not simply a tool for communication but it supports us in our everyday life and it is also a "tool" in our professional dealings at work, to give us information and knowledge to help us make more informed decisions better and faster. This technological advancement affects not only our individual lives but also structures in which companies and even the global economy cooperate and collaborate.

Communicating relevant, mission-critical information is an indispensable task in today's work environment as well as in our private lives. Success is in part based on how much knowledge we have, which itself ultimately depends on how we communicate and how fast we process information.

In the past few decades, for both our professional and private lives, we communicated using media such as paper and pen, typewriter, and the phone. In the business environment, the use of paper to communicate with companies outside caused vast quantities of paper to be transported over long routes, which resulted in long waiting times and inefficient flow of information. Introduction of the early phone system helped to greatly increase efficiency but was subject to the limited availability of the intermediate connector to the other party and allowed only audio data to be transferred. The inability to transfer other forms of data such as documents, screenshots, or other contextual information is a limitation when you are only able to communicate by audio.

This, however, does not mean that individuals or companies in the past were inefficient and unsuccessful because they were unable to communicate the way we are doing today. Being "successful" is a temporary condition, which once reached, does not automatically continue for a team or an individual. Success is the result of a consistent investment in the uniqueness of the company or of the individual, the use of performance-relevant core competencies, and the ability to learn faster than others and to change in a broader sense. The right strategies, visions, mission statements, organizational structures, competent managers, and especially employees are important for success. But correct and relevant information to make sound and informed decisions helps the organization to be continually successful. Thus, the critical role is to look into ways employees, departments, offices, and business partners communicate and collaborate with one another.

Fundamentally, basic communication, as you can imagine, is the basis for all these forms of modern communication and collaboration to take place. In order to better understand current and future possibilities for communication and collaboration let me first take you back once again to the past.

What changed the communication industry?

In the past few decades, a technical change took place due to the changing conditions and requirements of information processing with the need to communicate and collaborate in our global economy.

In addition to globalization, an important benefit for business was also created by countless technical developments. For example, the invention of the Internet was considered one of the biggest changes in the information community since the invention of the printing press. The initial networking of universities and research institutes which later spread into the commercial sector, and eventually to the private sector, had an unexpected impact on various areas of everyday life. In 1990, the Internet was given virtually free by the US National Science Foundation to the world as a communication network for various technology companies, research institutes, and universities to develop. The following diagram illustrates the development of telecommunication since the mid-eighteenth century and the innovations that were invented with software-based technology. In other words, traditional telecommunication- and software-based communication and collaboration technologies are coming closer together, merging and building a strong convergence for the future.

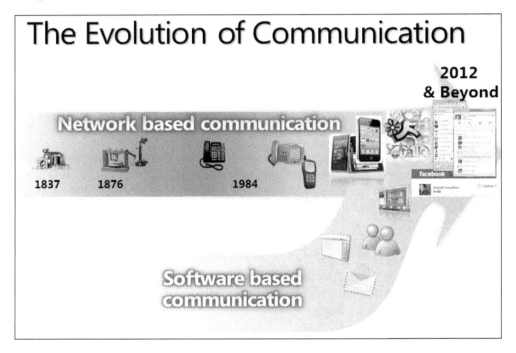

Technological development of the Internet also created changing conditions in the market economy. Initially, these new possibilities on the part of many companies were more or less declared as "utopia" or only short-term achievement.

The initial technology was available but insufficient to provide a real benefit for companies. However, in 1993, through the development of new communication protocols by Tim Berners-Lee (who is considered the inventor of the World Wide Web and the HTTP protocol) and CERN, there was a rapid boost of the Internet by increasing the efficient exchange of information.

E-mail as a carrier of information in business and for private users was usable with these extensions and innovations of the Internet. On closer inspection, the exchange of information via e-mail probably created the first milestone for trends such as the "paperless office", to create savings in shipping and telephone costs.

Understanding modern business communication needs

Today, e-mail is not a trend but an established type of communication that is deeply integrated with our communication and business processes. Although "paperless office" and telephone cost savings using this technology have been realized, communication in companies significantly increased because you spend less time and less cost to transport information from point A to point B.

What is the relationship between technologies, such as the Internet, e-mail, and the phone and the information processing and collaboration for businesses?

The very same question is asked; how can we make cooperation within and outside companies more efficient?

How can we communicate easier and quicker? Can companies achieve their goals more easily with these tools? Are there ways to avoid/reduce costs to increase savings? Can we make it easier to deal with this knowledge change? What potential gains and advantages exist here for the companies? What kind of changes will we need in the company and how will the changes affect the person who has to implement them? How can in-house projects be realized in order to improve the communication?

To answer these questions, it is important to look at the communication trends in recent years. In the past five to ten years, with combined usage of previously developed and established milestones in communication technology, the Internet and the telephone, we were able to benefit from efficient client information while constantly developing communication technology.

Wi-Fi, which has only existed for several years as a standard in companies and in public places such as airports, cafes, and so on, is now used by nearly all mobile communications devices. Wi-Fi allows us to communicate with words and images wirelessly to the Internet/local area network.

Computer Telephony Integration (CTI), fax, and voicemail are some of the basic terms that play a special role in cooperation and information processing.

The fact that almost every workplace has an Internet connection these days shows the need to simplify all communication possibilities for all users. This includes the Internet, e-mail, landline phones, mobile phones, video conferencing equipment, tablets, PCs, netbooks, and smartphones. It is important to highlight that connectivity to the Internet and telecommunication services is still a challenge in some areas of the world and even a luxury for some developed countries and regions. Even in these developed places we will find some remote locations with limited (slow) Internet connections.

More often than not, new software promising better benefits in communication and cooperation tends to overwhelm employees in the company. Year after year, companies have invested over and over again in new technologies trying to get a competitive edge over other companies, by improving their internal processes and procedures through more efficient communication methods or technologies.

In the past few years, the number and complexity of technologies and processes has escalated so much that these developments and investments are showing signs of having a negative impact on the efficiency and effectiveness of the company.

Also, many business owners believed that pure investment in new tools, new software programs, and new communication equipment is the sole solution for better structural communication. This circumstance is still one of the top challenges and problems for IT and change processes in organizations.

Since the 1990s, according to international studies (such as the Federal Reserve Board of Governors) a large percentage of the available budget is used for communications and information technologies.

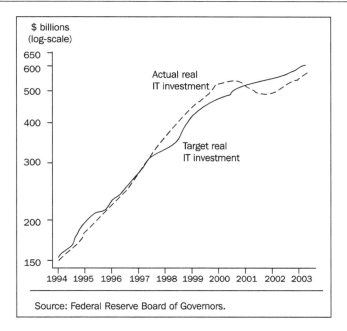

$ billions
(log-scale)

Actual real
IT investment

Target real
IT investment

1994 1995 1996 1997 1998 1999 2000 2001 2002 2003

Source: Federal Reserve Board of Governors.

The chart shows that companies are continuously upgrading and investing in their technology. Even though the study begun in the last century, it is a fact that this same development has progressed to today. Through the investments made, it is obvious that IT investments are an above-average priority for many companies.

The dotted line "Actual real IT investment" shows the IT investments *realized* in the North American region, the solid line "Target real IT investment" shows, on the other hand, the "target" IT investment is based on financial planning and forecasting of organizations.

In the other chapters of this book, we will specifically focus on the "pure" IT investments (which are the actual IT investments). Through more expensive investments in information and communication technology, we will be able to see clearly that we need more than a wealth of different complex technologies to communicate and collaborate amongst employees, customers, partner companies, and so on.

Precisely for this reason, software and technology companies that were developed a few years ago started implementing solutions in this field of communications so that technology "should unify the main day-to-day communication tools".

Evolution of communication tools

The old wired phone of the past has evolved over the years to include more uses and functionalities, and has been transformed into today's phone, which is effectively a mobile communication link. A telephone using its own PBX (Private Branch Exchange = Telephony system) in the company is very different from a modern mobile phone with the integrated mobile phone operator services.

Global companies led the integration of different technologies to improve communication. Internal studies and analyses that were conducted showed that the average employee uses many devices such as a PC, a work phone (landline), possibly several mobile phones, a tablet, a fax, a notebook, and/or a Netbook.

Perhaps you can still remember the "Pager", which was expensive when released but has long since been replaced by innovations from the mobile industry (excluding a few regions and certain professional areas such as the hospitals that are still using pagers for urgent communication).

Of course, such studies on consumer communication are not solely used to find out the number of devices per user, but other important data such as the frequency and intensity of usage on the various devices so that companies can invest in the appropriate technology and the staff to facilitate communication and collaboration with others.

Such studies revealed high costs for the workplace equipment and loss of efficiency was caused by an overlap and a "flood" of technologies. Due to this confusion of numerous devices and their associated communication chaos, many companies have invested increasingly in the so-called unified messaging solutions. The focus of such solutions is to provide individual employees a standardized tool to carry out their job functions more efficiently.

This represents a portion of unified messaging known as CTI, as mentioned earlier. CTI solutions are a specialized kind of software which is used for the integration of workplace phones into workstation software solutions such as Microsoft Office and Exchange, Lotus Notes, Novell GroupWise, or others. A use case scenario could be a PC with Microsoft Outlook installed, where an information worker can click to call from an e-mail or from the address book and also use basic CTI features such as to put the call into a conference call, put a call on hold, or forward and hang up a call.

The goal of unified messaging solutions is to take the load of the various complex technologies away so that we could communicate rapidly and efficiently manage human resources within the business.

CTI-solutions linked to telecommunications with the electronic data processing allows functionalities such as adoption, termination, and the automatic dial-up telephone calls from a personal computer (PC) to be possible.

Fax and voicemail are also part of unified messaging. Electronic fax can be dispatched and received from any workstation. Voicemails can take and playback voice messages using unified messaging applications.

By using these solutions there is not only comprehensive efficiency but also cost saving without investing in more new telephone systems, add-ons (plugins), proprietary software, fax machines, telephones, and more.

However, the integration solved the problems of unified messaging applications and technologies only partially because there are more and more new communication possibilities existing within the company, on the Internet with additional phone numbers, e-mail addresses, and various web communication options.

Increasing the number of ways to reach a person

The number of communication possibilities a person can have grows significantly to be complex. To illustrate this, let me use my fictitious business cards to show you a small example of today's available communication avenues.

Do you see the problem that arises when there are many different accessibility options?

```
Daniel Jonathan Valik

Sr. Program Manager – Unified Communications
Main:       +1 (425) 9999-991      Facebook: Daniel Jonathan Valik
Direct:     +1 (425) 9999-992      Xing: Daniel Jonathan Valik
Mobile:     +1 (425) 9999-993      Linkedin: Daniel Jonathan Valik
Home:       +1 (425) 9999-994      Live Space: www.DJV.com
Assistant: +1 (425) 9999-995       UC Blog: www.technet.com
Pager:      +1 (425) 9999-996
Fax:        +1 (425) 9999-997

Business E-Mail: davalik@microsoft.com    Personal Email: Daniel.Valik@Live.com
Business IM: davalik@microsoft.com        Personal IM: Daniel.Valik@Messengeruser.com
WEB: www.Microsoft.com

Microsoft Cooperation
```

We know that the trend of communication has changed considerably and is still undergoing change. A software solution without integration into specific business processes and activities will not provide a competitive advantage. Overall, unified messaging is an interesting and rather innovative approach of simplifying communication tools.

Since 2000, new possibilities for digital collaboration have been developed based on previous experiences and these should benefit not only technical areas in companies but should also be adapted into the business processes and goals of the company to produce real and measurable value.

Among these new possibilities, in addition to the previously mentioned unified messaging technologies, there is **Voice over Internet Protocol (VoIP)** telephony, intelligent intranet and Internet platforms, collaboration portals, instant messaging solutions, IP video conferencing, and presence integration (which provides the availability information of the employees, customers, partners, and so on).

The relevance of "support business processes" with technology optimized for the end user has become clear to the solution providers and technology vendors. This rethinking is motivated by the increased competition, the need to increase profit margins, and problems of market growth in the global economy. In the process of unifying communications, more and more thoughts from a technical perspective are incorporated into the concept of unified messaging and telephony/mobile telephony.

Benefits of UC

Unified communications offers a measurable benefit for companies by value-enhancing usage to allow easy communication combined with simultaneous exchange of information among users in their daily communication.

To further explain the term **unified communications** (UC) at this point, the word unified means to bring everything together in **real-time communication** (RTC). In contrast to unified messaging (integration of telephony, fax, and voicemail), the idea behind unified communications is a merger of all available communications services, especially instant messaging systems (which are the integration with presence features) to facilitate the accessibility of communication partners.

The further integration of this technology in our work and business processes is an important focus and also an increasingly frequent request to the technology vendors and manufacturers. Unified communications can be understood as an extension of unified messaging because unified messaging refers to the integration of messages in an application and is in fact a form of asynchronous communication. Unified communications takes this a step further to create real-time communication as it aims to integrate synchronous communication media together.

Also note that the possibilities of unified communication from the portal and social networking platform technologies have also increased. You will certainly have heard of Google+, Netlog, SkyDrive, Facebook, Twitter, LinkedIn, XING, and other platforms. These platforms allow not only the exchange of personal and business-related information, but also the integration and availability of further real time communication and collaboration add-ons like instant messaging, document-sharing, Internet telephony and even integration with line of business applications.

We do not only focus on the way information within the companies is changing but also we have to keep an eye on how the consumer environment is changing. The integration of such services has shifted from a pure consumer to a business or consumer/business mixed variant and very often, communication with business and private contacts overlap.

Let's take a look at Facebook. Facebook created at first a social networking platform to give people the opportunity to get connected, exchange content like pictures, personal information, friend lists, and more. Several years later, Facebook created a new platform inside the original Facebook application with the name Branchout. Branchout's idea was derived from Facebook. Branchout sets out to provide similar features to Facebook but for business. The idea is comparable to other social networks like Linkedin or XING where people get connected, create business, or find jobs and career opportunities. With Branchout, Facebook went into a more business related and focused area — integrated in the private social network.

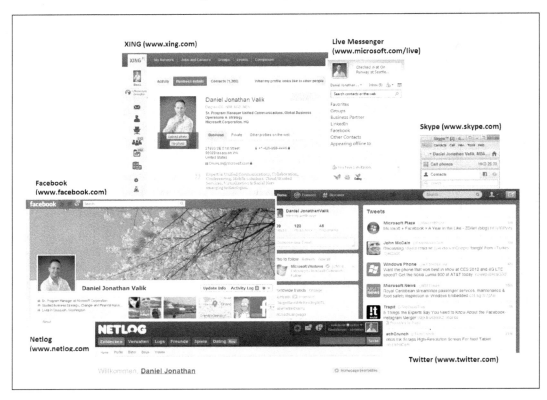

Social networks offer an important platform for product information and sales. International studies have shown that in the future, more products and services through social networks and platforms can be distributed and rated, just like departmental stores or shops.

The technology allows us to communicate with "friends" and contacts about the quality of the product and to write a review providing information on the product. This is only one example of social networks. Another good example is product marketing. How companies provide information about their services and products changed completely with the development of social networks. Facebook, Twitter, LinkedIn, Amazon, Google, Microsoft, and other companies changed how customers receive information when shopping for products and services. The technology trend is clear: this change will continue. Online shops, marketing, and access to products and service information through social networks will be the standard for the new generation of end users and buyers.

Other trends include increased networking with business applications for companies. Many manufacturers and software companies also increasingly offer their solutions to integrate and coexist with social platforms. For example, Microsoft, Cisco, and IBM offer networking with Facebook and other social networks in its collaboration solutions. They are simplified to integrate communication, information, and contact databases. It will be no surprise that solutions available on the desktop and office computers will also be further extended to mobile devices such as tablets in the near future.

Introducing cloud services in IT and telecommunication

The next most obvious immediate change in IT and telecommunications is cloud services, or even cloud computing. Many of the aforementioned communication solutions and social networks are pure "cloud" solutions.

But what exactly does this mean? At this point, I would like to give a rough overview of the solutions-based cloud and its conceptual idea first and revisit it in more detail again in the later chapters.

Cloud is comparable to hosted and provided services with IT and telecommunications solutions. Cloud offers "computing" in the form of a service.

Cloud services by global providers are not the "typical" new IT solution as cloud offers complete integration or a combination of cloud with the IT environment and needs of a company. In other words, cloud services are theoretically accessible from any device and platforms and also the actual computing power is provided centrally in the cloud.

In addition, user data or other information is located in the cloud, so PCs, tablets, or mobile devices tap into the cloud-based applications like how we get our utilities such as electricity and water from a central supply.

Another advantage is that the cloud has a simple solution-based offering, at least for most common services like e-mail, social media, or basic real-time collaboration, so it requires no special knowledge to get the actual services to work/operate. When we talk about the cloud, it is important to differentiate the several different types of cloud computing. There is the "consumer cloud", which usually offers free or inexpensive communication, collaboration, e-mail services, data storage solutions, and many others. Then there is the business cloud. The business cloud computing offers small, medium, and enterprise companies a variety of different services and technologies that are usually not free and also need more planning before they can be used for business purposes. Anyone who dives into the field of business cloud services will very quickly recognize that the core concept of these services is not new at all. For many years, companies always had the choice to invest in their own IT, telecommunications services, data, storage, security, and also web services. The alternative is "hosted services" offered to business customers by companies like IBM, Verizon, and AT&T. The evolution of cloud computing is in reality the convergence of hosted services into cloud computing — in other words, hosting 2.0.

With cloud computing for business customers, we no longer talk about having specific cloud services that are not working properly or have temporarily disrupted services. They have high service level agreements between the business customers and the provider of cloud computing solutions. Companies usually think about cloud computing, and transferring or merging their current in-house solutions and IT platforms to cloud services due to one or more of the following reasons:

- Need to save cost and to reduce IT and telecommunication equipment inside the company.

- High **Return On Investment (ROI)** when investing in cloud computing compared to the traditional in-house solutions.

- Pay only for the actual use. For example, data storage – how much hosted storage space is needed? E-mail services – how many mailboxes, what size and configuration are required?

- More effective outsourcing strategy and not be dependent on only one provider (cloud services can be migrated quickly between different providers if required).

- Less need to invest and upgrade IT and telecommunication technology for the company. In other words, the upgrade cycle and need for an investment on this is practically not required anymore.

- Hand over the IT and telecommunications services to a provider who is specialist in it as it is not our core competency.

- Want to concentrate on core competencies and drive innovations faster in order to have a faster "time to market" for their own product or service.

These reasons given are usually for business justification when planning for cloud computing. Some of today's cloud services even migrate from the consumer space into the business area. An example is the company Dropbox (`www.dropbox.com`), which offers a free service for consumers to store photos, documents, music, videos, and other content easily into the cloud. Dropbox was founded in 2007 by Drew Houston and Arash Ferdowsi, two students from MIT (Massachusetts Institute of Technology), who invented the idea of this service when they started e-mailing files to themselves from home to work and to more than one computer. The idea of Dropbox was born.

Another example is Microsoft's SkyDrive, which offers consumers not only storage but also e-mail services, sharing and security options between multiple devices and technology, the automated synchronization of selected folders between multiple devices, and much more. Microsoft and Dropbox are not the only ones offering such services. What we see is that consumer cloud services can also be extended for business purposes. This is probably the case for many different technology areas and even the choice of devices and operation system platform.

The following graphic illustrates some key areas and advantages for centralized cloud services:

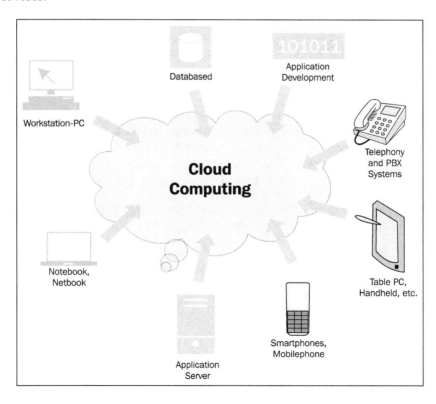

Internet and connected technologies will continue to undergo rapid changes with advancing technology. We can only vaguely dream how and what we will use to communicate, cooperate, and conduct information exchanges twenty to thirty years from now.

On the whole, it is obvious that traditional IT and telecommunication will move towards cloud computing or a form of cloud hybrid implementation and usage of technology services. When we look back to this point in time in the future, we might remember the emergence of cloud technology as the first step into a different world of technology and services. Just like how the first mobile phone or Internet was developed and changed the way we communicate, share information, and even how we purchase services today.

If you compare a telecommunication provider's traditional service and their present day service, it is important to recognize that the business model of such companies has changed and will continue to dramatically change in the next few years.

It is not only important to offer minutes and data bandwidth to customers; it will be important to understand the customers' business and business requirements but also their communication, collaboration, and cloud strategy. Only with this level of attention and partnership, will it be possible to stay in the market and grow from a business perspective together with technological changes, especially in the areas of communication and collaboration. We would look into cost advantages in unified communications and its cloud services options in the later chapters.

Summary

The field of **unified communications & collaboration** (UCC) and social networking arose from the global trend of devising new methods using new technologies to allow cooperation between employees, customers, partners, corporate collaborations, networks alliances, and economic interactions between business organizations.

In addition to these new collaboration opportunities, UCC offers increasingly sustainable cost savings for organizations utilizing cloud services. Cloud service is an alternative to the standard IT environment and could perhaps lead the emergence towards the next new standard.

The drive to improve as an individual and organization supports all of these innovations to the next stages of development, which is to make it easier to transfer information among the recipients. Thus, technological and organizational structures will become an even more relevant and decisive competitive factor in the future.

However, unified communications, collaboration, or social networks would be just another technical invention or additional terminologies if not used efficiently for communication, information exchange, or in areas of knowledge or cooperation management.

You will learn in the next chapters the benefits and potential for success from unified communications using these technologies.

2

Information Technology Meets Knowledge Management

What forces are driving the changes in communication and cooperation in society? Is the thirst for knowledge responsible for such developments? Let's start with a basic analysis of why knowledge is important. In order to survive, every living thing has to have the knowledge to carry out necessary activities such as searching for food, protecting its territory, and protecting itself. This, in a way, ensures the future generation of its kind. Knowledge provides security. A more complex form of knowledge such as experience takes more time to acquire and is the accumulation of the learning of knowledge.

Knowledge in an organization is the sum of all the individual knowledge of the people who are in the organization. Strange as it may seem, the amount of knowledge per employee when averaged out is relatively the same across all companies in the world.

We recognize that knowledge is necessary and through its individual employees, the organization is able to tap into the various elements to create success. Maximizing each employee's knowledge base is becoming an increasing priority for organizations. At the same time, globalization has brought us closer towards information- and knowledge-based activities. Knowledge is thus one of the fundamental building blocks we need to have on our road to success.

Consistent learning is the only way to improve ourselves, help us gain a competitive advantage, and use it to gain recognition and be successful.

Several studies support these global developments and project similar trends for the future. InformationWeek 6/2007 confirms these developments and they are projected to continue over the next few years.

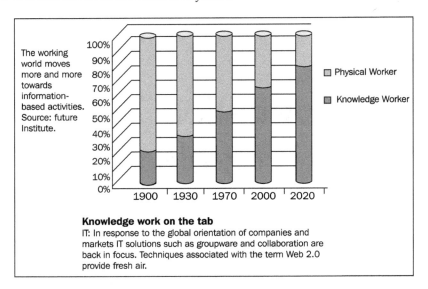

The working world moves more and more towards information-based activities. Source: future Institute.

Knowledge work on the tab
IT: In response to the global orientation of companies and markets IT solutions such as groupware and collaboration are back in focus. Techniques associated with the term Web 2.0 provide fresh air.

Introduction of modern technology and electronics has affected many processes and is largely responsible for the increased learning pace in our lives today. The Internet has improved distribution channels and a better storage medium has made access to explicit knowledge increasingly easier.

Before the Internet and many other technologies found their way into companies, all the information was stored as data in folders and shelves in the office. It was difficult and time-consuming, and hence costly to accumulate information and this information could not be easily accessed by employees.

In the modern computer age, information can be stored in a more productive and economical means by having data virtually stored in the "library" of the company as data files on the computer.

The trend in Web 2.0 (or perhaps in Web 3.0 and above by the time you read this book) and future technologies like cloud services reveal new possibilities for storing knowledge on the "global" database of the Internet.

In view of the global nature of businesses and markets, IT solutions such as Groupware (for further information and explanation go to http://en.wikipedia.org/wiki/Groupware) bring collaboration back into focus due to the increase in knowledge work. This breath of fresh air provides techniques that are associated with the Web buzzword: physical worker and knowledge worker.

Since communication and cooperation began, new technologies were developed to allow us to process information more easily. Companies that use technology have correspondingly more advantages over companies that do not.

As we know, information technology has made the handling of information and knowledge simpler, among other things. This in turn gave rise to another interesting topic of knowledge management.

Information technology is used to support knowledge work in general or the market economy. For example, e-mail attempts to solve more or less the same problem of filing information that has been used for years in business communication.

Similarly, documentation, presentation materials, and internal documents are stored in a larger variety of systems, tools, file servers (electronic filing technology), and on the intranet or the Internet. Because of this complexity and lack of transparency, it is no longer as clear if information technology has created a real advantage or not. Entrepreneurs believed that through the use of knowledge management, we are able to rely on "helpful" technology to achieve more productivity and have better benefits.

The past here also shows that investing in expensive IT solutions and software-based storage systems resulted in an ergonomically poor system and did not bring about the benefits of actual knowledge management in organizations. Knowledge management was largely confused with information management because it follows the same original idea which is to increase the productivity and efficiency in the company. The amount of information increases rapidly and this puts pressure on the employees to make use of this information using current technologies.

As mentioned previously, knowledge holds the keys to success. In most cases it is very important to have the right level of information to work on specific processes, create content, work with customers and partners, or fulfill other key areas of work. To access information, understand it quickly, and to include that into the daily workflow is a very important competitive advantage. However, the application and selection of truly relevant and necessary knowledge is an absolute prerequisite. In most organizations, we find that information is stored in an unstructured manner in various systems and the amount of information processed daily goes well beyond the processing volume of an individual employee.

It is necessary for us to process data and information daily in order to acquire new factual, procedural, and implicit knowledge in our work and everyday lives. However, not all the information that we have is necessary for us to effectively work and make decisions. As a result, it is important that organizations and enterprises capture this knowledge using good information technology systems in order to develop and distribute the truly relevant information.

What could be the ultimate advantage in the correct use of technologies in the field of knowledge management? It has been proven that the correct use of technical instruments is a critical factor for successful knowledge management. The management of knowledge refers not only to the structure and its application, but also ways to positively influence individuals, which in turn increases the knowledge base of companies. The knowledge base here refers to all data and information from all levels of the organization. It gives an organization the ability to find solutions for tasks and problematic situations.

Today's IT systems have a lot more advantages as compared to the simple filing systems of the past. They are not limited to only file servers or databases, in which documents and information are stored, but also set trends in communications technology, the exchange of knowledge in new areas, and to boost efficiency. We are talking about "unified communications and collaboration" in technology, communication, and cooperation as discussed in the previous chapter and here again in knowledge management with correct supporting applications.

After 90 years of research and development in manufacturing technology, software industry companies such as Microsoft, Cisco, IBM, EMC, SAP, and many more, have started developing new technologies such as web applications, groupware solutions, enterprise content management solutions, and workflow/process-oriented software products that facilitate the management of "collaboration". To facilitate the knowledge and information exchange among businesses, various manufacturers have a variety of approaches in the pursuit of solutions for cooperation and collaboration in order to achieve *asynchronous processing of information*.

A concrete example is the Microsoft Office solution suite. Microsoft SharePoint is one of the platforms that offers benefits for several collaboration scenarios and not just for data centers; it also has a cloud solution in the Microsoft Office 365 suite. In these solutions, via a portal, there is a targeted figure and distribution of individual and organizational knowledge in the areas of business intelligence, communities, business processes and forms, enterprise content management, enterprise search, and collaboration of information among different teams and different independent companies.

Microsoft SharePoint offers the great ability to create personalized websites (My Site) for employees inside an organization.

Microsoft SharePoint Server as a knowledge platform

Microsoft's SharePoint Server can be used in implementation of the so-called workflows in organizations. Workflows can be defined, documented, and supported by information technology. An employee can input certain customer information into the system so that another department will have access to this same information necessary for the next steps within the same project. These inputs, best practices, or lessons learned could be collected and then put into a **Community of Practice (CoP)**, so that an incoming telephone call from a particular customer can be directed to the right contact at the company immediately. This would not have been possible without the intervention of such technology. It is no longer necessary for employees to have a holding queue for incoming calls. Even when an employee goes on holiday or a new employee takes over, the software system will be able to help ensure that the original desired workflow process can be easily executed. Microsoft SharePoint Server is thus suited ideally for efficient knowledge workflows. See the previous screenshot for a knowledge platform which can be used to collect, transport, and to expand its statistics data map or be kept in the company archives as explicit knowledge.

Another example is that Microsoft SharePoint Server can be used as a library of knowledge. The following image shows SharePoint Server used as a question/answer (FAQ) system and explicitly used as a best practices database that can be searched by the user for specific information and extensions of opportunity through the posted knowledge. In this example, Microsoft SharePoint provides the user with a list of important documents and content and even functions as a platform for discussions and posting.

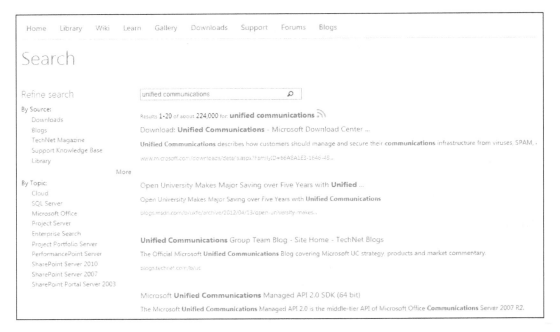

Microsoft SharePoint Server is a great platform for knowledge sharing and collaboration inside an organization and with external organizations.

Microsoft SharePoint as FAQ, collaboration, and best practice platform

This differs from the earlier concept of "unified communications and collaborations" of efficient communication in real-time information exchange. Unified communication is in the field of knowledge management as the IT solution's knowledge and information exchange center.

UC affects the strategy implemented within a company. Although it is technology, it can affect the financial strategy of the company. The field of knowledge utilization, availability, and especially the documentation of knowledge affects how people in the company make decisions and this also affects the financial strategy in the end. In other words, to think about knowledge management and to develop this into an integral aspect of the organization is a necessary success factor. As part of the knowledge management it is further important to think about the "people to document" strategies and technologies inside the company's environment. When used wisely, it can also be used for people development within the organization.

We have previous examples from the Microsoft SharePoint Server where the promotion of personal communication among employees is made possible and easier. This is known as "person to person" strategy and is the anchoring area for the technological solution for unified communications today. Various technology companies compete directly or are in cooperation with one another to offer solutions to achieve "synchronous communication" such as video conferencing equipment, VoIP telephony, video entertainment, availability information integration (presence integration), instant messaging (text-based, real-time communications), and much more.

Communication and cooperation is able to improve the productivity of employees in various companies. Many case studies, for example from leading research companies like Gartner, Forrester, IDC, and others conducted disproved the widely held assumption that **instant messaging (IM)** or other IT solutions in this busy environment during working hours were disruptive in terms of effective work hours and distracted employees from their duties.

Several case studies have found that the usage of IM services and other real-time communication technologies did not interrupt the "daily work" of employees but the usage actually increased the performance and effectiveness at work.

The explanation for this is that IM replaces or reduces the information from the other usual forms of communication such as telephone or e-mail. It helped the employee to quickly select which relevant information needs support. Through the use of instant messaging technologies, according to recent studies it also reduces the time needed for communicative understanding and this gives the users more time to focus on their core tasks.

A particular international study of the Ohio State University (www.osu.edu) and the University of California (www.uci.edu) demonstrated the efficiency of communication and collaboration technologies and the following advantage for communication inside and outside the company's boundaries.

A very high percentage of the total 912 full-time workers surveyed understood that the IM is not for private chats but is used for business communication. Additionally, full-time workers provided the feedback that IM is an ideal type of communication to keep in contact with coworkers and customers.

Through this study it became apparent that employees who use IM think very strategically and are selective and efficient in communication. When it comes to the availability of possibilities, as explained earlier, many businesses are in competition with one another. Microsoft, Cisco, IBM, Google, Salesforce.com, Apple, and other software companies offer software to store information and knowledge in high-tech facilities to ultimately allow real-time communication.

The rapid development in the online sector is a growing business potential for electronic support for knowledge management. Examples include the Microsoft Office Communications Server 2007 R2, the new Microsoft Lync Server, all real-time communication (synchronous communication) such as IM, VoIP (Voice over Internet Protocol), and audio and video conferencing for businesses. VoIP delivers voice packages over a specific network layer. Many different technologies use VoIP integration to offer "network" and "Internet telephony" to end users. Specifically, to Microsoft Office Communications Server and Lync Server, the system works in conjunction with existing telecommunications systems or IP carrier "Trunks" (IP connection by service provider/carrier) and allows the companies which are set up on these phone networks to use the latest VoIP conferencing options.

The Microsoft Lync Server is also used for the integration of presence information, a key advantage of unified communications and collaboration provided by Microsoft. The system allows users to actively communicate, share, and easily use information or knowledge with other users or employees within a company and connected business partners.

With regards to knowledge management, this software solution allows the user to first and foremost have a visual representation of his/her contacts, so this gives accessibility for the creation of discussion forums and group. The user may choose to communicate with others using various real-time communication options such as a simple phone call, IM, or a technical professional videoconferencing.

Another interesting feature is the integration of systems; for example, a video conference could be recorded on any portal from other manufacturers or on the Microsoft SharePoint Server so that knowledge can be stored and saved for distribution. The use of software solutions such as Microsoft Lync Server or Microsoft SharePoint Server allows the stored knowledge to be used later in completely new aspects, allowing knowledge management to be efficiently integrated into work processes of organizations or companies. Instead of writing documentation or instructions via email to other team members or directly to customers, employees may record then post a short video or voice information on the intranet using SharePoint.

Like many companies, colleges and universities have also made use of such communication and cooperation technologies to implement and put together e-learning for their students. This is comparable to the idea of web technology with real-time communication and the familiar YouTube Internet site. Although the published home videos on YouTube may seem to have little to do with your daily business, when it is consumed daily by many millions of people, this information might become important for commercial purposes. If you look at companies, it is obvious that platforms or portals like YouTube can be extremely useful in training user groups, IT administrators, information workers, or informing customers about new products and services, and sharing information about them. It is also natural for services like YouTube to step into the business environment to beneficially share information and content inside an organization, between business partners and of course, among customers.

YouTube offers the possibility to upload videos for use as learning content, product presentations, recorded events, and conferences, and also as a platform for marketing new products and services.

YouTube as a video knowledge portal

This is then clear that having an integrated business solution that allows real-time streaming of data, having the ability to share videos, documents, or forms within your company and with business partners via the SharePoint site would be in the same way advantageous for everyone at work. The portal technology is also helpful to transport information and knowledge content that have data size too large to be sent by conventional e-mail.

This integrated solution is not just limited to web technologies but it should be accessible anywhere in the world from one's personal laptop, netbook, tablet PC, or traditional personal computer (PC) and workstation. Hence it is important to select the *right* technology so that all mobile devices such as iPhone/iPad from Apple or devices running on Microsoft's Windows Phone, Blackberry's RIM, or Google's Android can be integrated into the business and be compatible with the base system that the company uses.

For example, Microsoft has a technologically secure solution that allows knowledge management (SharePoint integration) or real-time communications (presence information, IM, or for example video conferencing) using the Windows Phone. This solution can also be extended to devices from other leading companies such as Apple, Cisco, and Google for better integration capabilities so that their devices can serve as multifunctional devices. At this point it is also important to highlight that Microsoft Lync 2013 offers a great integration of real-time communication with mobile devices like the Windows Phone and other platforms. It is also possible to initiate a video conference very easily by a click, see if other contacts inside and outside the organization are "available", and also contact them via IM. Implementation of communication features on the mobile device is just the first step. In the same way, Microsoft SharePoint offers a very close integration with mobile devices and brings collaboration features (combined with the communication modalities as mentioned before) to almost any mobile platform. With these technologies, it is now easy to provide access to information, to share knowledge among the information workers, and combine communication features like IM, video, among others on top of this integration.

As you can see, efficient technology is not only used in supporting daily work but it offers many new and innovative ways to process information and knowledge. We could have a team collaboration portal or website set up for the purpose of sharing employee-related information like the Microsoft team portal in which all teams and staff have accesses to a company-wide intranet to search for information, exchange information, and news.

The following graphics and screenshots illustrate a company's central intranet portal and team sites that can be generated and hosted with Microsoft SharePoint technology:

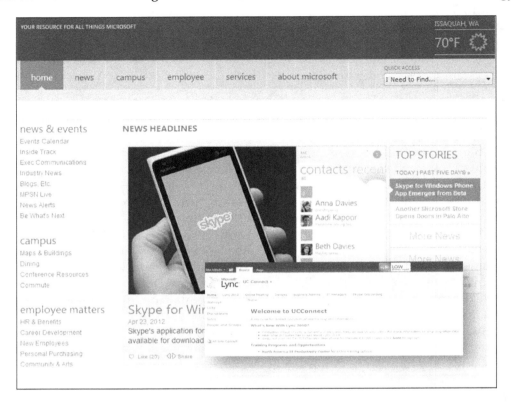

A company's central intranet portal and team sites on Microsoft SharePoint

Another central and important role in this communication platform is the presence of suppliers. All conversations from the suppliers are linked to the same profile information in the address book, that is, complete presence (online/offline status) information with all the different ways that are available to contact the person. This method of communication is like other similar products such as Microsoft Skype, Microsoft Live Messenger, Yahoo Messenger, AOL Messenger, Skype, ICQ, Tencent QQ, and so on.

With publicly available communication platforms, we also see other collaboration technologies that are "free for use" in the World Wide Web. The distinguishing difference between Internet-offered solutions and applications such as Microsoft SharePoint or SAP is the ability to integrate with other enterprise applications and information security, and that the exchange of knowledge and information cannot be accessed without authorization. The Internet offers a wide set of solutions and software platforms that can be used to collaborate and communicate with end customers. The important point is to always concentrate on business requirements and to select the "right" platform for the business. In other words, if a small or mid-sized company uses a freeware or open source platform without any specific service level agreements or foundation to extend the platform for future requirements, this could be the right step to quickly provide some sort of communication and collaboration to the business.

However, it is very important to think about the level of integration and collaboration into other lines of business applications, how users will use the platform inside the company, outside the company, on mobile devices, security issues, restrictions for both internal users and external users and of course, integration of real-time communication technologies such as IM, presence information, and more. As mentioned before, it would be easier to have a Microsoft SharePoint team site and see if team members are available or not, and to have the ability to click on a specific contact and choose the method of communication (click to call, video, or audio conference).

The following images illustrate the integration and the need for real-time communication that should be part of any team site and company's intranet site. Again we use the power of unified communications. With Lync 2013, it is possible to develop a solid communication infrastructure easily for any SharePoint site or portal. In this example, it would be a great user case for team sites and web portals to share information and knowledge with business partners and to communicate with the author of a specific Microsoft PowerPoint or Word documentation.

Another example is the ability to access a document on a SharePoint site, click on a button, and share the document via a real-time meeting with a new team member. There are many different ways to use knowledge and information more efficiently. To be fair, there are many technologies other than Microsoft on the market. Similar solutions are Cisco's WebEx Social (formerly Cisco Quad) collaboration technology, Cisco Unified Presence server, IBM Lotus Notes, and Sametime. In our example, we concentrate on Microsoft SharePoint and Lync but more importantly, knowledge management is a part of the company's "content" strategy and there must be enough financial support to select the "right" tools and technologies. Having knowledge management inside the company is important and it gives employees and individuals enough resources to use, develop, and learn from the published content.

It is also important to have the best available technology based on the business requirements to resolve the technological problem of "how to access information" inside and outside the organization. At this point, it is also important to highlight that there are many other scenarios where you can use a collaboration platform like Microsoft's SharePoint or Cisco's WebEx Social (Quad) solution. Other examples would be the use for specific project and communication workflows, internal processes inside the company such as vacation request, timesheets, learning portal, personal website, and many others. In addition, more and more "free" product solutions are found on the web for businesses to support and encourage the exchange of knowledge. You might have guessed it already by now, a very good example of knowledge portal on the web is Wikipedia (www.wikipedia.com) which allows user search and is supported in many different languages. Users are able to input new knowledge and share it with the world using this site. Although Wikipedia is not exactly an ideal solution for enterprise company information, this platform can be used to search for knowledge and can also be extended to real enterprise solutions and portals.

The following image illustrates Microsoft Lync 2013 for Windows, Mac, and other platforms, which is a great and efficient real-time communication platform as well as a knowledge and content platform together with Microsoft SharePoint.

Microsoft Lync 2013 and its capabilities: IM, VoIP, information sharing, and video conferencing for several different platforms:

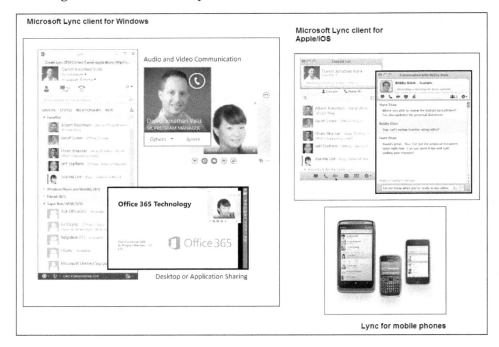

From skill search and real-time communication to mobile integration

Unified communication technologies (such as Lync for different software platforms) show some of the different ways in which communication, collaboration, and knowledge sharing can be promoted in enterprises. Next to the Microsoft Collaboration suite you will find many other efficient and intelligent solutions that can support the transfer and exchange of knowledge in an organization.

To support knowledge management and information processing requires an understanding of how companies use knowledge, which knowledge sources are present in the organization, and which forms of knowledge between employees, departments, divisions, and corporate offices is processed. There must be an understanding of the company so that there is no arbitrary information technology invested. Technology is a critical support tool that has huge potential to improve the overall output of the organization and company.

Knowledge as strength is increasingly short-lived as it gets much faster to receive, process, and distribute information in the future. The technology is here to stay and help us to be smarter and more efficient. It will only get more and more efficient for us to search and get information in the future.

As companies of the future get more intelligent with more knowledge, knowledge management will be the next economic consideration for companies. The company needs to make the best decisions and strategies against its global competitors and be in alignment with the company's goals and mission statements.

Summary

Knowledge management is an indispensable and strategic operational issue for companies today. Knowledge is one of the most important keys to making creative, intelligent, and useful products for the customer and is also needed to stay competitive. This is clearly not only for organizations but also for every individual. Each of us gains knowledge everyday, developing continuously and "selling" knowledge to our customers and to our company.

Modern information and communication technology has taken important steps to support the goals of today's knowledge-based enterprises. Although information technology only represents one of the components of knowledge management, it is definitely a not-to-be-missed success factor.

This topic of collaboration and communication at the technological level is the same for all the different technological companies, although it may be marketed in different forms. Whether it is Microsoft, Cisco, IBM, Google, Apple, or any other corporation who owns the new technology in the future, it is important that this advancement is able to enable us to communicate and work more easily, both in our professional and private lives.

Information technology will continue to be an important factor in knowledge management so that knowledge can be exchanged and communicated globally.

In the next chapter, you will learn about how knowledge and communication can be shared and established between different organizations.

3
Business Cooperation in the World of the World Wide Web

The complexity and speed of today's market economy requires the optimization of operations and requires you to consider partnerships in order to gain competitiveness in time and other potential advantages. Since the last century, the way in which we work and how companies operate in the market has changed fundamentally.

In the past, companies used to create, develop, and align their potentials with the organization's mission statement over a specific time (mostly long-term). A company that has more efficient employees simply produced more, enabling the company to gain more profits and reach its targets. This positions the company for success. Today, these factors are still as important.

However, in the past, the main focus of companies was to retain independence and to safeguard their own enterprise and investment. Rarely these independent companies unite to form a cooperation that has a common business goal.

A company in the technical market would try to gain economic success alone by increasing its revenue, achieving growth by introducing innovative and intelligent products and by marketing these products as economically as possible.

The late 1970s and early 1980s were deeply aggravated by global competition, which correspondingly influenced a company's strategic approach to market penetration. Companies recognized that having strategic cooperation with independent enterprises can bring about a reduction of some business uncertainties, giving them better competitive robustness. In the 1990s, more and more business cooperations and corporate networks were set up to be more effective, promoting cooperation.

Globalization has led to the transformation of our society towards a knowledge society. At the same time, increased cost and time pressures, and resource scarcity have changed the usual corporate-owned culture. Economic unions and organizational structures became necessary. To remain successful among today's competition, it is important to focus on sharing innovation, market strength, skills, and resources within the enterprise. Many examples show that corporate partnerships, networks, alliances, virtual enterprises, joint ventures, and other forms of cooperation today are no longer rare and in most cases, a company's success is now a joint responsibility.

What are the reasons for rethinking how organizations cooperate? One of the main reasons is the changing circumstances caused by increased globalization, as mentioned earlier, and the internationalization of companies. "Globalization" is a term that came about in the 1990s and it is used to describe the international economic actions of companies to make use of global common resources and skills.

Another important reason for the cooperation transformation is the aggravated competition at the international level, which could lead to the risk of market saturation. The development of global markets has forced companies to compete globally as well as in national and regional markets on cost, time, quality, and price. This increases the complexity in all areas of the economic union. The following figure summarizes the main interests for business cooperation.

In recent times, joint ventures alliances, business networks, and many other forms of corporate cross-cooperation gained at the global, international, and national level are gaining more importance.

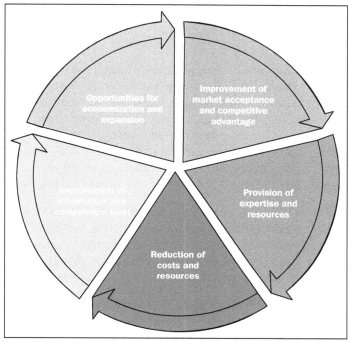

The benefits of business partnerships

In addition to the rapid changes in the business environment, advances in information and communication technology have progressed faster than ever before. The immediate worldwide availability of news and information has created a transparent global market. Internet and telecommunication allowed economic transactions to be conducted from anywhere in the world. The trade transaction of goods at low cost is accelerated by this development. Money and capital markets changed radically because electronic commerce can be bought and sold at any time of day. Thus, news on a shortage of petroleum or certain foods can result in a prompt increase in commodity prices and affect other markets (for example, the automotive industry) within a short period of time.

This shows that information technology has directly influenced the strategic approach in global business. However, which of these technologies can be used to support the strategic and operational cooperation between companies? Corporate collaborations and networks are usually representations of strategic decisions of corporate management. Hence, such changes businesses also require changes in how an organization is connected. Among these changes, there would probably be cultural, structural adjustments in internal and external communication that would affect employees, customers, and partners, product and service adjustments (for example, joint research, development, and so on), and technological "barriers" of cooperating businesses.

What technological barriers are we talking about?

When two or more organizations come together and decide to create a company-wide cooperation, especially in the very advanced stages of this cooperation, the information technology structure and systems design are significantly important. To ensure the success of this cooperation, both companies should identify, adapt, and adopt important technologies to allow both companies the required access to the shared information (CRM data, skill, resource databases, and so on). It is no longer a rarity that in such alliances, employees have access to the other company's information in order to have a more efficient work relationship.

Most IT applications available generally use common file and storage servers, web platforms, CRM systems, ERP systems, web portals, e-mail servers, electronic address books, and calendar information to create a joint communication and collaboration system. This cooperation and collaboration design in the information and communication technology is maintained in almost all sectors of the economy.

In previous chapters, we have discussed the advantages of unified communication (UC), how UC has influenced the field of knowledge management, how it could make cooperation and communication more efficient, and how it could be a key success factor, particularly in inter-company cooperation. The following pages will focus on detailed IT solutions that the IT industry uses within corporate partnerships.

In the last few years, there have been substantial changes in the exchange and communication of business information. In the earlier days of IT, limited technical capabilities, like minimal data bandwidth of the Internet, have created a sort of barrier in the exchange of information between different users within an organization or technological networks, hence making it impossible to support collaboration between two cooperating companies efficiently. With the continuous development of IT, many possible different technical solutions are now available.

The availability of such integration solutions brings about another key concern in IT, that is, the security of your data. Since the beginning of 2000, as the Internet became more efficient, new security software services have started emerging rapidly. Communication and information exchange across the globe between people and companies became easier and is now the norm. Such developments created new trends and insights into security, and sometimes an obsession about security in the company due to circulating news about data security breaches in the public, government, and banking sectors from time to time. Encryption of business concepts or safety-critical applications that require a secure data exchange over the "free" Internet is not an efficient solution for a security-conscious company. It has become an important issue for these companies to keep technical systems that are used to store numerous encrypted algorithms safe.

This brings us back to the global demand on efficient communication and collaboration technologies, which fuel an important issue-solving approach in unified communications.

Understanding the unified communications umbrella

Unified communications is an umbrella term that covers the technical aspects in communications and collaboration. In other words, unified communications offer all relevant modalities to simplify and promote information exchange within business partnerships.

Let's shift focus onto the costs involved in running a cooperation. We have IT, project management, external/internal mentoring/coaching, communication and travel costs, and so on. These are also areas in which unified communications can be applied. For example, the exchange of information for each and every meeting can be conducted more efficiently and this eliminates the need to travel and also reduces the cost of calls for the company. Another example for the great use of unified communications technology and its related **Return of Investment (ROI)** is to convert internal and external announcements, employee trainings, or even company events to online meetings. This not only saves time, it makes it possible to communicate information across all time zones more easily and faster. Many international companies use UC, for example Microsoft Lync or Cisco's UC tools and applications for all kinds of collaboration inside the organization and with business partners and customers. For some VIP customers, it is common to invest in full communications and collaboration-enabled meeting rooms, where a conference can be held in full HD (High Definition quality) audio and video among all parties.

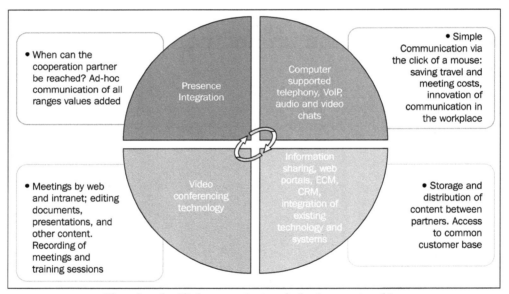

The value of unified communications for business partnerships

As mentioned before, unified communications is an umbrella term for **Integrated Communication Technology (ICT)** and real-time communication. However, various manufacturers have coined this term differently for their own portfolio of solutions. Some may prefer the term collaboration, unified messaging e-collaboration, unified technology or the more common term, unified communication, we are still talking about the same improvements in internal/global collaboration and communication.

This is very interesting, especially in collaborations because without much planning effort, company-wide communication is possible. However, with this there are also disadvantages, such as there being no secured channel for communication between partners without centralized IT control. Each user has the technical capabilities to communicate and transfer company information to partners over unsecured lines. Some businesses, such as the banks or finance departments in companies, are good examples of where they need to have highly secure areas that have control of the information that is exchanged using modern tools and communication modalities like IM or data sharing with Dropbox, Microsoft SkyDrive, Microsoft SharePoint, or Cisco WebEx Social (Quad).

One enterprise solution provided by Cisco allows other services including IM, video conferencing integration, web conferencing integration, presence and social networking integration, in addition to telephone integration in a VoIP environment, and other services. This is similar to another solution provided by IBM Technology Group known as "Lotus Sametime" and "LotusLive", which offers the communication technologies mentioned earlier together with an e-mail and collaboration platform. Microsoft, another software manufacturer, offers the same solution with focus on communication and collaboration. The advantage of the Microsoft solution platform is the ability to be integrated with software products and technologies from other manufacturers. Another advantage of Microsoft's solution is the ability to implement a high level of security into the UC platform. With SSL data encryption, secure certificates, and additional security options it is possible to make every instant message or audio and video call more secure. Security is of course not only an important issue for Microsoft; Cisco, IBM, and many others have similar or different security mechanisms in their UC product stacks and platforms, but based on "easy ways to implement" Microsoft perhaps offers one of the great advantages in this area.

Microsoft's solution platform can be adapted and designed according to customer's requirements with or without development effort. An example for standard integration is to design Lync 2013 based on all business-required communication features and implement the communication servers in the IT environment of the company. Depending on their needs, whether only internal, or both internal and external communication, and the collaboration that is needed, the complexity in the design of the UC platform changes. Areas where development would probably be required is if a company decides to integrate diverse line of business applications (LOB applications) like CRM, advanced reporting and business intelligence tools, or also custom applications together with the UC solution. An example is the use of unified communications in contact center projects, where Microsoft Lync or Cisco's Unified Presence solution is integrated into a complex communications and collaboration workflow from customers to support agents. The development of such extensive use cases for unified communications should not be shocking at this point. It needs to be seen as a great advantage for the unified communications platform.

Let us look at the various models of the Microsoft UC solution. As mentioned in the previous chapter, Microsoft offers their solution in two different options to customers: "On-Premise" (which is integrated in the customer's own data center) or as a "Cloud Service" (where the software is a service). For companies which are working as partners in cooperation with one another, as mentioned before, they could use their Microsoft SharePoint solution for this. Via Microsoft SharePoint, it would be possible to store relevant information in a web application so that each partner has a "safe" way to have access to the needed information. This information is usually stored in the Microsoft SQL Server, an extremely high performance database solution compared to other solutions in the IT market.

Learning about My Site

The SharePoint Server is used in cooperation as "My Site" for employees of the respective companies, ex-Nortel (now part of Nortel belongs to Avaya), or the HP-Microsoft alliance.

My Site is a personalized "home page" that gives you a central location to manage and store your documents, content, links, and contacts of each partner and via the intranet and the Internet with appropriate integration; it can be used to locate specific information for individual employees. In this scenario, business cooperation could for example, be advantageous when it is possible to contact a person in a particular business unit from other companies.

My Site is able to store documents from an employee or integrate the presence information of a person or the whole team to the rest of the organization. It is also possible to publish the position of a person as part of the hierarchy structure inside the company or it can be used to publish the current project with all necessary information. Content providers can use My Site as a method of customizing the information they present to users.

The ability to share necessary information on this structured surface gives such cooperating companies an enormous advantage because employees from these companies can work more efficiently by optimizing their time.

The following is an example of a personal web portal created on My Site:

With various permission settings, users within and outside an organization (for example, field service, mobile employees) are able to access desired information or related external information.

Instant messaging and chat

The second part of the Microsoft solution platform (unified communications) is a basic variant which allows IM communication between the respective partners. IM provides a comfortable advantage because instead of generating cost and intense telephone conversations, "short messages" can be exchanged efficiently. Since IM is a well-known type of real-time communication, it is important to highlight that there are many different ways IM and chat can be used. For example, IM can be integrated in the form of persistent chat or also as "IM robot" instead of the traditional 1:1 and 1: many communications. IM can also be used as a conversation translator or as a automated workflow among different communication parties. Persistent chat, for example, would be a great tool if one person needs to communicate with several different partners but does not wish to set up an IM conference; it would be possible to open a chat room, post questions, talk about different topics, and then search through the conversation history at a later time. Persistent chat is in other words the integration of IM in an asynchronous way.

Instant messaging or chat is an extremely important way to communicate across organizational boundaries or across different technologies' boundaries, such as a "chat" between Microsoft Lync and Skype. In many areas of business, more and more telephony systems are converting to IM and chat. Of course, the use of IM technology is closely linked to the type of business and the communication culture with customers and business partners. International studies from Gartner, Forrester, IDC, and others have shown that chat is a mandatory modality for real-time communications and in some ways, it is also because we have a generation of people who have grown up with diverse IM tools and technologies. Besides chat, presence information is also a very important factor. Before a chat is established with someone, it is important to know if the person is actually available for the conversation. When we want to speak to another person in a different organization or company which is in partnership with our company, it is even more important to select the "right" time for a conversation about specific topics and content.

The following screenshot illustrates an example where the Microsoft solution platform is used in partnerships such as Microsoft and Polycom alliance. It shows the ability of this platform to communicate with many other selected and *affiliated* companies, to create contact lists, and to share your availability status with other parties.

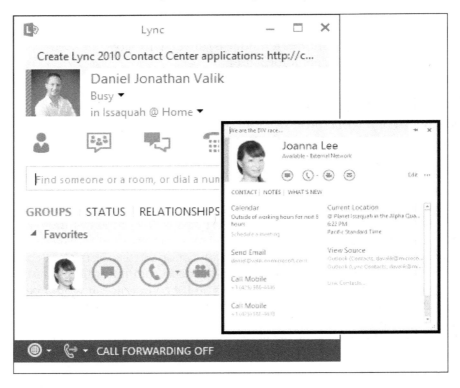

Another possible phase of expansion is the integration of telephony in the various software applications in the company. Since in any cooperative relationship, the company always has various different software applications, it is important to evaluate whether the selected unified communications solution is compatible with existing applications.

There would be an efficiency disadvantage and waste in resources if two partners invest in an IT solution but only one of the companies has the technical requirements to achieve the desired communication and collaboration.

The advantage of such phone integrations is the simplification of phone functionalities (redirection, call forwarding, call waiting, ad-hoc conferences, scheduled meetings, and so on) into a simple visual display on the workstation computer. A user in company A might reach the desired contact in company B using a simple search in a central corporate address book and mouse click on the contact to call. This is also a very good example of "calling" a social contact instead of using a phone number. The contact information of both parties could be part of a central address book and it stores not only the number but it also has their full name, your social contact to that specific person, relationship status (business, friend, family, and so on), or the level of the business partnership. This concept for company to company communication can be easily archived with a Lync Federation where both companies can access contact and personal information of employees in the other company.

Technically, this scenario can also be integrated with the existing telephone or on a VoIP phone or headset (a connected headset on the phone or the personal computer). An advantage for such a system is when employees who are outside the office premises and are on the **Public Switched Telephone Network (PSTN)** are able to make calls using their office numbers. The modern technical interfaces to the respective corporate IT allows all communication options, including telephony, to be used from outside the company. Usually an employee needs to be in the company to use the telephony system for inbound and outbound calls but with unified communications and the integration of VoIP, it is possible for employees who are using the application to have a have a softphone with the associated office phone number. This is a great advantage when employees are working from home or when a business travel is required. This is demonstrated in the following "working from home" scenario. With unified communications, it is possible that the home office has the same integration with the company-wide telecommunication system as the actual office. The availability of VoIP integration is also a great cost advantage. By configuring routing mechanisms and software-based rules, international calls can take the best and most inexpensive route through selected carriers or unified communications breakout points.

Global businesses now have the ability to save a part of their telephony cost using this technology or Lync Federation (which is the best option to optimize cost) and these technologies deliver great business value. Telephony integration can also be implemented in different ways. A company could use their existing telecommunication environment for this or a carrier could host the "PBX" (Private Branch Exchange or Telephony system) for the company and offer the required interfaces for further extension to a unified communications platform. However, the UC piece could also be part of a hosted offering from well-known carriers such as Verizon, AT&T, CenturyLink, Telefonica, and many others internationally. Another cost saving point is that employees do not need the traditional desk phone anymore and are even more productive with mobile headsets, handsets, or bluetooth devices connected to their softphone on different platforms like tablets, smartphones, or other equipment. The cost saving and optimization factors for UC and VoIP will be further explained in *Chapter 5, Cost Optimization Approaches*.

In the following screenshot, you can see the integration of telephony systems in Microsoft Lync Server:

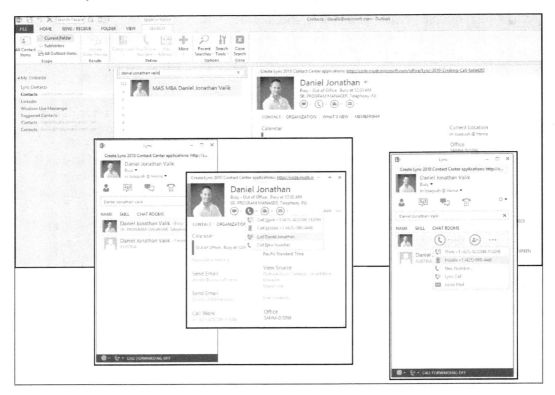

The support of modern technology with another important building block, video conferencing technology, could facilitate cultural and information exchange in meetings between companies. These companies could now more easily have business corporations that exist in different parts of the country or different parts of the world. Video conferencing between two businesses is not the only example. Video conferencing used as a daily communication modality saves time and provides sometimes more comfort and other advantages over a phone call or an instant message. In many worldwide businesses, it is absolutely necessary to offer video conferencing to employees, business partners, and customers to establish the business ecosystem and to transfer information quickly from one location to another. With solutions such as ICQ, Skype, Live Messenger, Google talk, Apple FaceTime, and many others, it is obvious that real-time communication, which includes video conferencing, has spread from homes back to businesses. Several studies predicted that video conferencing will be a standard communication modality for every business in a couple of years from now. The question is "Why do I need to see the other person" will be obsolete, it is even more important to integrate video conferencing into mobile services, kiosks for customer care or perhaps shops in a mall if you want to purchase a product or talk to the manager who is not physically in the shop.

One more reason for video conferencing technologies is again cost-saving through the cost of travel activities and actual communication for the companies' collaboration. This is especially important after the financial crisis and economic changes in recent years. These unified communications and collaboration solutions saved high proportions of travel expenses by converting necessary meetings and travels for the business into online meetings or video conferences. Video conferencing is also very comfortable and useful because you can see the immediate reaction of the person you are speaking to during a conversation. For negotiations, sales, or product support, this could be a differentiating factor for a successful outcome.

Let me provide you an example at this point; business partnerships which are located in two different locations in Europe have realized technology projects together simply by using the unified communications and collaborations solution as their communication tool. In this example, one company offered the "federation" through the unified communications platform to the other company and through audio and video conferencing it was easy to do recurring project meetings online instead of traveling back and forth between the locations of both companies or to have high charges for telephony cost on both sides. From telephony integration to video conferencing (online meetings) to Lync Federation, these are great cost saving and optimization opportunities.

Knowing the modular IT platform

Another possible variant solution is a modular design of the unified communications platform. Besides the previously mentioned features like VoIP/telephony integration, the Microsoft Unified Communications platform can additionally be supplemented by video conference integration. This module can be integrated as an option in the Lync Server. This also means that existing video conferencing systems from manufacturers such as Polycom, Hewlett-Packard, Tandberg (Cisco), Sony, LifeSize, or the new Microsoft video conferencing room systems can be implemented. This is an important ROI factor, because video conferencing rooms or media rooms are usually a very high investment and can easily scale up from a couple of thousand USD to half a million or more.

With the extension of the video conferencing capability of the Unified Communications platform and softphone application on the user's device or desktop, a user can initiate and plan a video or audio meeting conference and send invites out electronically via e-mail in a cooperating company. This is not only used in the previously mentioned client application; it can also be used in conference rooms and media rooms as "video endpoints" in the integration with Microsoft Lync. In a conference, sound, images, and any content such as presentations, documents, or spreadsheets on the Internet or on a common secure connection between the companies may be transferred. For this it is again very useful to plan for a secure connection between the businesses because no one wants to find, for example the financial report of a company on a Facebook wall or an Internet blog. The sound and images capability is also interesting when it comes to training as meetings and presentations videos can be recorded for easy playback. This can serve as a "meeting" database when implemented with a suitable filing system (such as the previously mentioned Microsoft SharePoint). Many international businesses record their meetings based on an archiving policy in their companies and it gives them the ability to access content after any conversation on a specific topic. However, laws and compliance rules are different from region to region. The "recording" of voice, video, and data can be a very sensitive topic. Back to the advantage of this technology: Employees who are part of specific projects could use the recording of video conferencing for documentation of specific projects between a business partner or a customer. Microsoft Lync offers an easy click-to-record feature which can be turned on during an audio or in this example, a video conference and can be also converted into a specific file format afterwards. For more information on recording technology, refer to *Chapter 2, Information Technology Meets Knowledge Management*.

The following screenshot is a video conference with multiple parties. It shows cooperating companies in the video and sound on the left-hand side. On the right-hand side of the screen, appropriate presentation materials (Microsoft PowerPoint Presentation) are transmitted for the meeting.

Summary

Any business can establish efficient joint cooperation, partnerships, and alliances with the support of unified communications and collaboration technologies. In this chapter, we have gone through the main advantages of all the communication and collaboration modalities for companies and their business partnerships or relationships with customers. In the world of today, it is extremely important to collaborate across the company's boundaries and to establish strategic partnership when needed. Unfortunately, they are sometimes not successful due to incorrect expectations and unexpected changes in the market.

However, as shown in this chapter, rapid exchange of relevant data and information is needed for the strategic and operational activities within corporate collaborations or networks. In the planning and implementation phase of such collaboration, each company needs to gather relevant information to decide whether or not a corporate cross-cooperation is actually necessary for them. In the past, communication and collaboration between partnering business also included expensive travel and phone costs to exchange information and to work together on projects. The world changed and real-time communication, social networking, cloud computing, and other new collaboration technologies are rapidly changing how we work together. In other words, the world is getting smaller and with all the mentioned advantages, it is possible to be more efficient and competitive in our daily business much more easily.

In the future, solutions described in this chapter will become even more increasingly relevant. Virtual companies will rely on these existing solutions or online solutions to work together and communicate for collaboration. More and more intelligent online services and so-called cloud services will offer similar features due to future technological trends in additional new opportunities for cooperation. With current development, the future might see the traditional telephony systems and equipment merge completely into cloud computing and services. Traditional telecommunication carriers may need to change their model into a data and line of business services offering. In this new future, it will be less important to bill for the number of minutes used per month on phone calls; it will be much more important to understand the customers' needs in terms of the business strategy and also the communication and collaboration strategy with their customers and business partner.

An example of a low cost online solution suite from Microsoft is Unified Communications @ Cloud services, which is under the umbrella of Office 365 or Lync online. The equivalent from IBM would be LotusLive and Cisco, which also offers a similar approach with WebEx and Unified Communications in the cloud.

Connecting businesses and individuals is an excellent example whereby technology today can change our daily work in a positive way to get closer to our environment for international cooperation and communication.

In the next few chapters, we will illustrate using the Microsoft solution portfolio where unified communications and collaboration are implemented in a variety of approaches. We will also highlight the advantages the end users will have in their daily business using the tools and communication technologies described here.

4
Value and Potential for End Users

After a Monday morning breakfast at home, I usually drive to my office, which is very close to the very nice area of Redmond, WA in the United States. As it is the usual morning rush hour to work for most people in the Microsoft town, it is a painfully slow journey along the roads. This happens when you work in an area where there are more than 45,000 people working for the same company. There are many useful technologies for intense waiting times like this, for example speech/voice recognition, mobile working/computing, and many others. When I arrive at the office, I turn on my laptop to check e-mails and upcoming events for the day. Most of the time, I find my schedule longer and more intensive than I would like it to be. In my Outlook mailbox, there are many new e-mails demanding my attention. As well as this, there are also many invitations for meetings, lunch meetings, coffee talks, and whatever the day brings. There could also be some important missed calls and invitations for telephone and video conferences.

Technology supports our daily life

Firstly, I call back customers and partners of important projects and issues. Instead of the usual fixed line phone, I pick up a new wireless headset and place it on my ear. With a simple mouse click, I open up my Microsoft Office Outlook and Lync as my personal unified communicator. In the past, at this point I would search for the contact from my Outlook Contacts list and dial the number on the keypad of my phone. As I often communicate with people internationally all over the world, I find myself mistyping once or twice before the call reaches the right person.

After I made my first phone call, I saw an incoming call from one of my important business partners, Mr. Thomas Schober from ACP Austria.

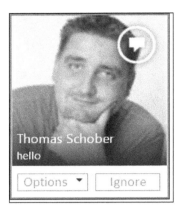

With another simple click, I am able to take the call from Thomas using my headset, and then my availability information is updated in my presence status as **In a call**, as shown in the following screenshot:

Why would this presence information be good while I am in a conversation? Well, I believe many of us have encountered this situation at one point or other where your colleagues or your boss sends you hundreds of instant messages, e-mails, or calls you while you are in an active conversation. Presence information can potentially save you from receiving such communication when you are already busy with a concurrent call or conference.

Back to the phone call. During this particular call, Thomas who is a Senior Architect and Project Manager for communication, collaboration, and infrastructure projects, wanted to have information on a few projects and certain documents. Unfortunately, I did not have them at hand or ready for this phone call. Because I knew that some other teams at Microsoft could help me with this, I told Thomas to wait a couple of seconds while I found the right resource for support. For this, I opened my Lync client and searched for my colleagues who could help me for that specific project documentation at Microsoft Redmond. The great point here is that when I use the Lync client's address book, I am able to do an integrated "skill search" to find a person based on their skill sets, specialties, or characteristics even when I do not know their names. Lync would return a list of people who fit my search inputs. This feature can be easily made possible when Lync and SharePoint are *integrated* with each other. I promptly found a colleague, Mr. Tim Karel, who on normal days would be just sitting 2 yards to the left of my desk at Microsoft.

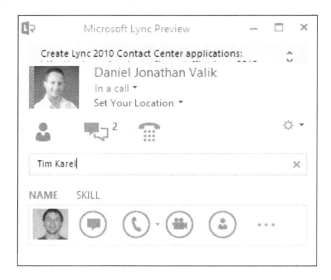

Using instant messaging, I found out that Tim is leaving for a meeting and I should ask another colleague and manager, Geoff Lowe, for the required documents instead. Again, via instant messaging I was able to communicate to Geoff that I needed the required documents. I promptly received his reply and with desktop sharing, I was able to show the documents to Thomas on my screen. As illustrated in the following screenshot, I am able to communicate with Thomas using Lync 2013, which offers communication modalities such as instant messaging, phone integration, sharing, and also great video conferencing integration.

A few years ago, I would have had to dial into a conference call with my username and a pass key (which was a very long identification number), which was sent originally to my e-mail address when I created the conference service account at Microsoft. Another possibility is to have a telephone conference on the good old phone. I used a very old gray scale display telephone set when I lived and worked in Western Europe and Southeast Asia. There is unfortunately a limited possible number of attendees when using the telephone system (Private Branch Exchange) for a conference.

Thanks to this communications solution, I am also able to drag-and-drop other colleagues like Joanna into my existing conversation with Thomas and we are able to discuss open points. After the call and a shot of espresso, I ran to the next meeting, an internal meeting in one of our conference rooms. Again, the purpose of the meeting was a customer project where **Microsoft Consulting Services** (**MCS**) and one of our business partners were involved. We would be able to discuss the project with all parties and especially with the business partner; I opened up my calendar schedule and with a mouse click on the **New Meeting** option in Outlook, I created a new "online" meeting and invited all attendees easily through e-mail.

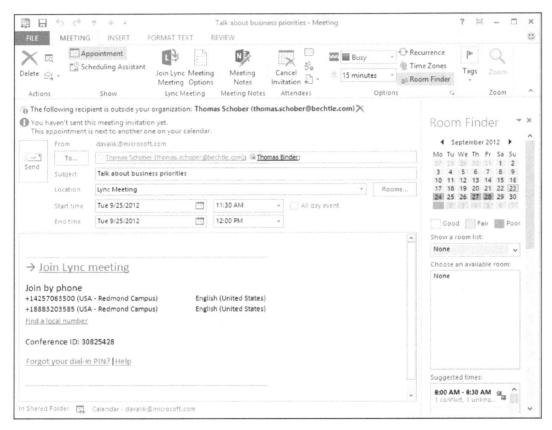

Shortly after all invited attendees have received the link for a video conference, they are able to click and join the conference. What a great and easy system! I am now able to have a conference with the customer, business partner, and some of my Microsoft colleagues. Because of the integrated webcam on my notebook, I was able to produce a high-definition video, took my certified Lync headset, and within 5 seconds was connected to everyone in an international video conference. With an additional click on **screen sharing**, I was able to add the required information of my Microsoft PowerPoint and Word documents into the conference and share it with everyone who needed to see the content during our discussion in the meeting.

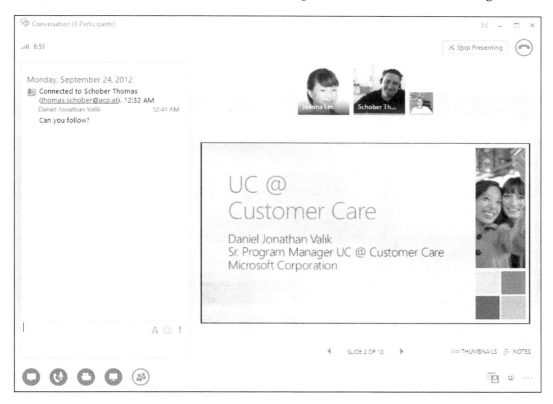

Persistent instant messaging

Another great way to communicate using Lync 2013 with people inside and outside the boundaries of their organization is through the use of Persistent Chat. You might have first known it as Group Chat; this is the former name used during the Office Communications Server 2007 (R2) period. Persistent Chat is real-time communication in chat rooms. This capability is already embedded in the Lync 2013 client application and is also available as a web client after some customization.

Whenever businesses, user groups, or communities need to have the ability to discuss a certain topic, search through chat history, collaborate in real time with a community, or have a place to discuss a specific topic, Persistent Chat is the right platform for connecting these people. It is important to understand the difference between "normal chat" and "persistent chat". A normal or standard chat would be between one or multiple people and the communicated content would also usually be saved as an archive. In Lync 2010 or Lync 2013 chat, it is simply saved as conversation history in Outlook. Persistent Chat offers the option, as mentioned in the previous chapter, to go to the next level and to create a chat room which stores the communication and exchanged content (for example, documents, web links, and so on) persistently in the chat room itself. With this integration, the user can open a chat room and can jump back to the previous conversation at any point in time. Another main differentiating point is that any "post" in a chat room that is published by another chat room member will create a notification that alerts all other chat room members about the new content.

In other words, with Persistent Chat we can take it a step further; we can create chat rooms for specific subject matters or for specific audiences. Let us say I invite Joanna and Thomas into a chat room called "Customer Project" and every time anyone posts or asks something in the chat room, everyone receives a notification from their Lync 2013 client. Users can be members of several chat rooms. They can either be configured as "Administrators" or as "Normal Users". When a user has the Administrator rights to a chat room, the user is then able to create, edit, or delete chat rooms and also invite other Administrators/chat room managers and other users into the room.

In many vertical businesses, Persistent Chat provides a great advantage. Let us consider the banking sector where a broker is able to share about a financial topic with everyone via Persistent Chat. All members in this chat room have real-time access to the result of this chat room discussion and are able to take the active role of communicating it back to their customers immediately. Another example that I have seen for the use of Persistent Chat is in the healthcare industry where doctors can engage in a chat room discussion about the treatment of a specific illness. For this particular scenario, I was involved in a customer project where Lync 2013 Persistent Chat was used to reduce the time needed to collaborate and communicate among several different special laboratories for a particular patient. The great advantage is that many ideas can come together quickly and the patient is able to receive a much better diagnosis and treatment, and thus a better service. Is this not a great tool for communication?

I have described parts of my hectic daily schedule to you earlier and I believe many of you reading would not want to have my schedule (hope I have gotten you to smile at this point). I have other examples which are closely related to my current work such as customer support, business development, product marketing, product strategy, and sales where Persistent Chat can make a difference.

In my daily life, I deal with many different projects around customer care and how to build better customer interfaces for supporting specific needs. Well, think about a scenario where a customer can open a web chat integration (via UC APIs) and be connected to a support agent who is there to resolve your problem and is at the same time connected to other specific expert chat rooms.

In another real life example, I led a project for one of Microsoft's businesses where the time needed to resolve each customer support case was strongly reduced, and achieved more than 43 percent ROI in the first year after the project was completed. We were able to save resources and increase the customer satisfaction for the overall support process.

Companies who offer any type of service or product are usually very concerned about their customer care strategy and this includes communication and collaboration with customers and business partners. An efficient customer care strategy and the use of an in-house or offshore customer contact center are absolute requirements to stay competitive with the other players on the market by offering quality support to customers.

In every contact center environment, support agents take calls, chat via instant messages, route customers to other experts such as Tier 2 or Tier 3 support level, and also involve and escalate support cases to their supervisors. Some of these resources might not be part of the same organization and because of this, cost efficient telecommunication or real-time communication is needed for these separate and independent contact center environments.

Persistent Chat can help modern contact centers establish better collaboration and communication among support agents, team managers, supervisors, and external resources. Another real example is an outsource contact center in Portland, Oregon, USA that offers dedicated support for consumer entertainment electronics and software. Customers have the option to connect to a support agent by phone or an optional web chat interface on the company's website. The support agent receives the inbound phone or chat notification on the desktop interface, and uses Lync and Persistent Chat to connect automatically to the right chat rooms based on the customer's selection of the required support area in the **Interactive Voice Response (IVR)** system or on the website itself.

Lync 2013 Persistent Chat for communication inside chat rooms

In this support scenario, the agent is able to connect to other support agents or specialists in the dedicated chat room to resolve the customer's inquiry in the fastest amount of time. An important goal in this scenario is to avoid transferring a customer or even making a call back to the customer from the support agents. In the event that a customer's inquiry needs to be transferred to another support resource, the next engaged agent would have access to the context of the problem situation through the chat history in the chat room.

Persistent Chat transforms customer care and offers a great new way of collaboration and communication among support resources. Here again, the benefit is the opportunity to save cost and increase customer satisfaction.

As illustrated in the previous example, Persistent Chat can help minimize the required time to connect to other human resources or even "robots" and "bots" in a chat room that may be part of the communication and collaboration strategy of an open customer case. By the way, a robot would be an example of an automated chat bot that answers questions through instant messaging or even voice response through a Lync 2013 chat conversation. There are many great examples of chat bots that are available and can be built into a Lync 2013 environment.

Persistent Chat not only aids in the reduction of time needed to resolve a case but also increases the overall customer satisfaction as well as helps to achieve high cost savings. Persistent Chat is an effective way for organizations to achieve an effective means of collaboration and communication with their customers, ensuring customer loyalty and a good reputation.

If you are interested in Persistent Chat, there are great add-ons available where a web chat integration or advanced business intelligence can be extended from the base installation of Lync 2013 Persistent Chat. Another important extension can be the integration of Lync 2013 Persistent Chat together with other line of business applications like **Customer Relationship Management** (CRM) software or customer ticketing systems. A good example here is the Formicary Collaboration Group (`www.fcg.im`), which has taken Lync 2013 Persistent Chat to a great new level with a wide expansion of the standard feature set into the Microsoft Outlook client, Apple IOS, Google Android, and of course Microsoft's Windows Phone. FCG also offers the extension of Lync Persistent Chat for Microsoft Outlook, the integration of CRM and other applications within Persistent Chat, and other extensions such as document and content sharing and social connectors (for Facebook, Twitter, Linkedin, and so on). In particular, the ability to combine information out of social networks into the Persistent Chat is a great example of bringing information together for specific use cases.

Imagine an online community where customers can ask a question and you can also query a search through the latest Linkedin posts or where posts from Facebook and Twitter or other websites get automatically included in the chat room. The customer could benefit from different information sources at the same time.

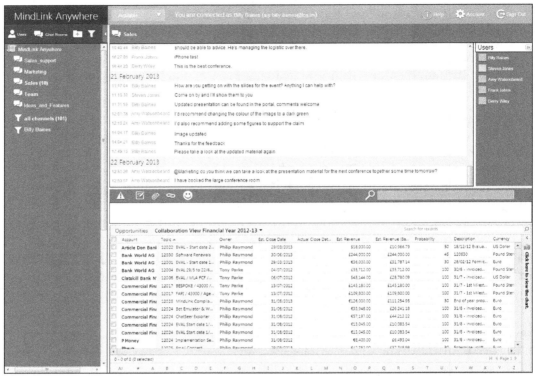

Formicary Collaboration Group (http://www.FCG.im) MindLink product – an integration of Lync Persistent Chat into a web browser interface with extended collaboration features and extension to Line of Business applications like CRM

Formicary Collaboration Group (http://www.FCG.im) MindLink product on a variety of different mobile platforms – Persistent Chat from everywhere

Being mobile – the mobility advantage

Let us go back to some other advantages of Lync 2013. On "office days" after lunch in the Microsoft canteen, I often go to the customers in the Seattle or Bellevue area to give presentations on topics such as the latest Lync Server, Lync and Skype in customer care and contact centers, Exchange Server, Social Networking, and/or cloud services news. At times, I have to participate in short, five-minute telephone conferences during the trip. Therefore, I take out my Windows Phone and select the option "Join Conference Call" from my mobile calendar. I am very happy with the simple and intuitive user interface of the Windows Phone 8, especially the easy connectivity of the mobile Lync client. I am definitely much happier with Windows Phone's new interface as compared to the older version of Windows Phone 6.5, which makes it difficult to just select the right calendar, appointment, or to communicate via e-mail or instant messaging.

After the audio conference, I was able to answer my colleague's short question about mobile devices via instant messaging on my phone. Thereafter I quickly switched back to the mobile calendar to see the next appointment and where I have to drive. The mobile integration provides a lot more features with the Lync 2013 client.

Like in the past I can easily join a conference with my other colleagues or with people outside my organization but with the Lync 2013 mobile version I can even join a video conference using my Windows, Android, or Apple phone. Of course, I could do the same on the tablet or any other mobile device. The great value of the mobile client is that I can use chat, change my presence information and availability, and video and audio through **Voice over Internet Protocol** (**VoIP**) easily from everywhere. Well, this makes the journey between the different Microsoft buildings in Redmond, Bellevue or journeys to and from business partners and customers across the Seattle area a lot easier and more efficient. The following screenshot provides some examples of Lync 2013 mobile integration across different devices and platforms:

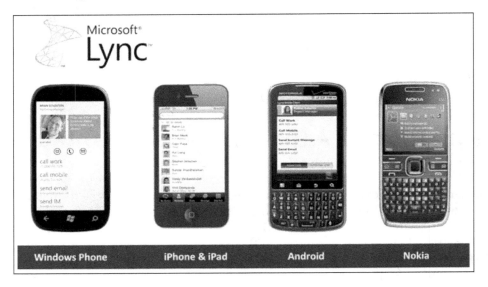

Mobility with Microsoft Lync has many different options. To bring it to the next level, you can easily connect Lync with certified conference devices to increase the quality of your online meeting or even use it to record training, speeches, and other type of presentations. The number of available devices and certified conference technologies for Lync has increased tremendously in the last couple of years (pretty much since Office Communications Server 2007 R2).

There are a couple of different options such as the Polycom CX5000, Microsoft's new conference room system – the Lync Room System, HP Halo system, Cisco Tandberg, and many others. On usual business days when I am back at the Microsoft office building from customer and partner meetings, I turn on my laptop again and with a USB connection to the Polycom CX5000 "RoundTable", I am able to start my next video conference or audio only conference.

From Roundtable and Email to CRM

The Polycom CX5000 "RoundTable" is a 360 degree panoramic video conferencing system. It has easy USB connection which can be connected to any PC running on Windows XP, Windows Vista, Windows 7, or Windows 8 to allow high-quality video conferencing with both picture and sound. Using Lync together with the RoundTable conferencing system, the customer is able to have a full panoramic view of all my colleagues without any required piece of software on their own personal computer or notebook. The great feature here is that the customer does not necessarily need to own Lync because he is able to participate as a guest with all the features. Using Lync, we were also able to record a video of our meeting and publish this on the SharePoint web space or site for the customers to download later as e-learning content. Other than CX5000 from Polycom, Jabra or Plantronics also offer many conference devices in many price ranges. The choice of devices for Lync 2013 can be found at `http://technet.microsoft.com/en-us/lync/gg278164.aspx`, as shown in the following screenshot:

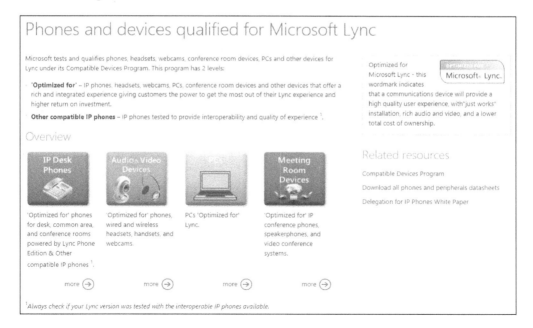

For my mobile meetings, I use Jabra SPEAK 510 and at home, I use Jabra Pro 9470 Bluetooth. When I am at the office or at a customer's/partner's site, I connect my Microsoft Surface (Pro) to a small conference device via a Bluetooth connection. When I am working from my home office, I start my home server and am connected to another type of Bluetooth headset for mobile working.

The Polycom CX5000 and Lync 2013 Gallery View and Panoramic Video is shown in the following screenshot:

The Panorama View example of Polycom CX5000 URL shown in the previous screenshot can be found at `http://blogs.technet.com/b/lync/archive/2012/10/15/lync-2013-videoconferencing-with-gallery-view.aspx`. The following image shows Jabra SPEAK 510 and Jabra Pro 9470 as Lync certified devices:

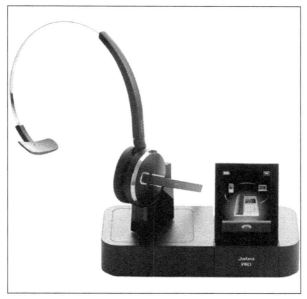

Using our Customer Relationship Database (Microsoft CRM/Dynamics technologies), which integrates with Microsoft Office, I am able to quickly retrieve information about the customer such as contract status, project status, or as part of unified communications, integration and availability (presence integration), which provides direct contact options such as voice and video calls or conferences. Since it is my job to drive Lync and Skype into the customer care field, there is a significant advantage of bringing real-time communication, collaboration, and a line of business applications such as CRM tools and applications together. When I work on different projects within Microsoft businesses or with customers outside the Microsoft Redmond area, I get a lot of interest from my businesses and customers when we talk about bringing a customer facing chat or click to connect option on a website and Microsoft CRM together into a single, fully-integrated communication workflow. The value that these technologies bring is the ability to recognize the customer on a different level, identify the customers' needs and serve all requirements at the end with much higher efficiency. Based on my experience driving projects with several international teams, I am able to conclude that most organizations have not integrated their communication technology into achieving a really good customer relationship management application or process. This is the reason why customers and partners around the world are looking out for people with this specialized experience to drive valuable CEBP workshops in their environment or together with selected customers.

At this point, I want to mention two projects that were implemented for Microsoft's businesses and are great reference examples for CRM integration projects. I was the project lead for these two projects and we have successfully achieved customer care and contact center integration using Lync 2013 as the platform. In these two projects, we have chosen to work with a solution partner of Microsoft, Clarity Connect.

If you are thinking of a better communication interface with customers and want to have CRM integration, Clarity Connect currently has the capabilities to bring these two areas together, professionally. In addition, Clarity Connect offers more features to manage an inbound customer call which is routed to a sales engineer in the company than you would have normally. They have extensions such as automated voice recording, pushing CRM workflows based on the type of customer, or the ability to manage specific activities out of CRM when integrating Lync and CRM together using Clarity Connect.

Another great example is Aspect, which offers a close integration of Lync 2013 together with CRM, SharePoint, and social media/social networking in a single user interface for sales or telesales resources. There are many other examples which could harness Aspect's technology to extend the capabilities of Lync in contact centers but we will discuss this topic again in a later chapter.

As you can see, using the right technology gives us a significant advantage in our daily work. The use of communication software in each company must be relevant to daily business needs. Generally, unified communications means that end users have integration in all possible stages. End users have e-mail, voice, and fax messages combined into a visible and workable universal inbox. It also means that communication options with a variety of devices such as a normal telephone set must have ease of usage and be available.

Behind the Microsoft unified communication solution, there are various required or optional building pieces, which were described in my typical daily business communication.

From e-mail to CRM, speech recognition and voice or video calls, unified communications offers end users great flexibility and mobility. Even though all described solutions are Microsoft products, it is important to highlight that there is a huge variety of solutions on the market. Other examples would include the platforms of Cisco, IBM, Oracle, Avaya, Google, Apple, and many other market players. The major importance of unified communication solutions is the integration into line of business applications or other network or application layer based integration. Why is this so important? Well, if the daily business requires "business" applications to be integrated with all communication tools, it is an added value for the end user and for the communication and collaboration inside and outside the company and for all other interactions. In the preceeding example, Microsoft Exchange Server, Lync Server, CRM, Office, and a telephone system (PBX) worked together to produce an overall solution that has great value in terms of time and cost savings. It is also a win for additional efficiency and possibly a higher competitive advantage for every information worker and the organization.

For the end users, it is critical that it has ease of usage when presence information, instant messaging, fax, voicemail, SMS, conference technology, phone functionality (CTI or enterprise voice, known as Voice over Internet Protocol — VoIP) and many other functions in the office are seamlessly integrated in such applications. Because of the interoperability in the overall solution, every user in various departments is able to work more closely together. This is an important aspect that needs to be considered in the selection of the technology used in real-time communication and collaboration.

Do more with real-time messaging

In unified communication technology, a message is made up of packets of information that are to be transferred. For this revolutionary simplification, messages could be transmitted in the form of e-mails, voicemails, phone calls, text messages, or instant messages. According to many studies in the IT sector, employees in companies today receive more than 100 messages a day through various channels. unified communications combines all of these communication channels in a solution so that efficiency and clarity of communication and information exchange can be substantially increased. It facilitates the management of contacts for the end user. In the previous chapters, I have shared with you that the central element of unified communication solution from Microsoft is the presence status, which is also available in Microsoft's free instant messaging products such as Live Messenger or also new in the product family, Skype (which is the replacement of Live Messenger). The user is able to see whether the desired communication partner is reachable or not, and which channels are available for connection. The user would be able to select the most optimal channel to communicate with other users. For example, a colleague is able to communicate easily with his colleague via instant messaging or phone calls. If making a phone call is preferred, it can be accomplished with one click using the VoIP connection over the Internet or a connected phone system(s). To bring together these different worlds, all the devices with different platforms need to be integrated to allow infrastructure and technology to be transferred. Using Lync Server, SharePoint Server, and Exchange Server, we are able to solve today's problem of having an explosion of infrastructure, devices, and all the applications and communication technologies that have accumulated in the last 10 to 20 years.

For the IT manager, this reduces the complexity and cost in implementing unified communications. They are able to transfer the integration task of the huge jungle of devices and applications to Microsoft's unified communications and collaboration platform. For the user, intuitive and efficient real-time contemporary cross-company communication that is adaptable to many different applications is now available through unified communications.

The great advantage of the unified communications platform

At this point, I would like to summarize the most important advantage of unified communications technologies: A single inbox that allows you access to everything; e-mail, voicemails, faxes, instant messaging, social networking components, and calendar events from your phones, computers, tablets, and any other devices in one single place. It also provides a seamless, user-friendly, and familiar interface across all devices to access your messages and to collaborate with customers or business partners.

Suddenly, videoconferencing with real-time documents or content sharing is not only possible, but even cheaper than a phone call and not to mention, the cost saving potential for business travels. When communication is faster and easier, it can significantly increase productivity and reduce travel costs.

A unified communication platform that integrates communication solutions, such as Microsoft Exchange Server and Microsoft Lync server into a single company-wide interface for all internal, customer, and business partner related interaction, makes employees not just more productive but also much more efficient. In other words, we could say that you are able to achieve more in less time and this is perhaps a key success factor in today's business world.

In summary, you no longer have to worry about disconnecting with your communication system. You can now work with a single system for e-mail, voicemail, mobile telephone, desktop telephone, and conferencing, plus its built-in protection functions for increased security, policy adherence, and ensured availability. If mobility is an important issue, the extension of communication and collaboration to any mobile device or platform is no longer a limitation of today's technology.

Technology saves cost and it increases efficiency inexpensively. It is easier to manage communications all within a common IT infrastructure. Most companies have their own infrastructure but with time we will see a change into having IT as a service solution, where infrastructure, communication, and collaboration are available as "cloud services" or hosted services.

Although the adaptation, extension, and line of business applications for unified communications are not available as ready to buy and install solutions in most cases, there are a variety of application interfaces in the server field and on the client side to allow expandability for almost every custom development. The following screenshot, of Lync 2013 development opportunities (`http://msdn.microsoft.com/en-us/library/lync/hh378554.aspx`), illustrates the Microsoft "UC" Developer Training Kit, which offers the ability to extend or implement most Lync 2013 modalities and features into other line of business applications:

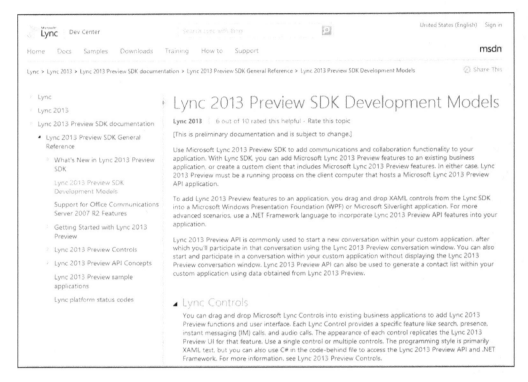

An important example for development opportunities is **Unified Communications Web App** (**UCWA**). With UCWA, it is possible to establish any web interface; in other words, any web browser can be used as a UC end point. This can be used in scenarios where you want to enable presence, chat, video, and audio communication (VoIP) and of course sharing only through the browser interface and without the need to install the Lync 2013 client. For businesses, this would mean that you can easily create a great web chat interface where customers can also have sharing or audio and video communication with federated resources inside the organization. Examples of departments which would benefit from this technology include customer support, sales, business development, or any other areas that need to have a seamless experience via all web browsers and interfaces. The following screenshot shows UCWA as a powerful new extension to the World Wide Web:

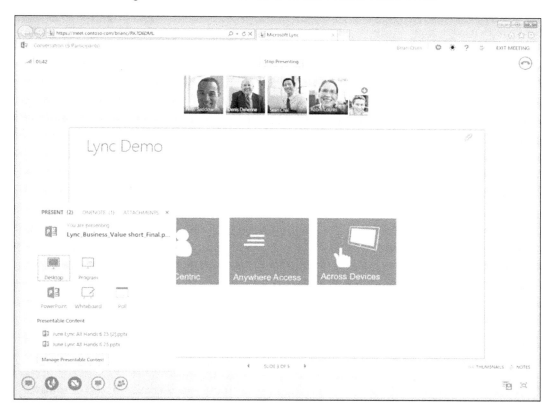

At the same time, all base parts of unified communications such as presence integration, instant messaging, and other communication modalities are not solely used in Microsoft Office or CRM environment. They may be mapped and can be integrated with little development effort (sometimes two lines of code) in applications such as SAP, other third-party CRM solutions, contact center platforms, company-wide line of business applications, IBM Lotus Notes, Apple IPhone/IPad, Google Android, RIM BlackBerry, web applications such as web sites, web portals, or more complex applications.

Developing your own UC add-ons

For Microsoft's Lync server, there is an easy to use and cost-free Lync **Server Developer Kit (SDK)**, **Unified Communications Managed API (UCMA)** – Lync and Speech Server API development package on Microsoft's website. In addition, the developer suite of tools such as Microsoft Visual Studio and even a telephone or face-to-face communication workflow can be designed in line with your business strategy to implement important steps such as enabling caller assignment to the next available employee.

More efficient custom extensions such as the Lync Automation API, Lync online meeting API, and Exchange Server Customization can be used to integrate the previously mentioned CRM or database applications or healthcare, customer care solutions, and many more **line-of-business (LOB)** applications in order to achieve a unified experience for end users.

The Microsoft Unified Communications suite offers intuitive and easy installation, integration, and administration for the IT and/or telecommunications departments and specialists. The Lync server is similar to the Exchange server or the SharePoint server and is divided into several functional roles, depending on the application stage, and how it is integrated into the corporate infrastructure. For example, a server role exists to integrate the PBX solution via ISDN or IP/SIP, another server role makes instant messaging, conferencing, audio-video communication, and presence integration with the backend systems possible and available. Of course, we will delve deeper into the technology in the next chapters but at this point, we have covered the high-level overview of the required infrastructure.

Last but not least, all solutions from Lync and Exchange to SharePoint, offer many deployment options, from a small and medium "standard" integration up to a highly available and enterprise-ready implementation, from cost efficient hardware, virtualization, and the option to run everything as a cloud service with the right choice of communication devices for the user—everything is ready.

For more information on solutions and technologies, you can refer to *Chapter 8, Technology Inside the Microsoft UC Platform and a Look into the Future.*

Summary

In this chapter, we covered daily communication and collaboration within an organization, with business partners and customers. We also talked about the broad set of certified Lync devices that are available in different price ranges and the need for these devices in professional Lync 2013 implementation projects and client rollouts. Lync 2013 also offers the great advantage to add/extend functionalities through custom development with APIs like UCMA or UCWA. From Lync 2013 Persistent Chat to the extension of many communication capabilities onto any mobile platform, Lync 2013 offers great value for an organization and for business-relevant communication and collaboration.

We also went through several different real-life examples in this chapter that illustrated the importance of communication technology for an organization as well as for an individual. We would also see consumer type tools like Skype slowly evolving into a daily business communication platform with customers and business partners around the world.

In this chapter, I talked about the "daily" routine of business that can be well-supported by this technology. What we would potentially see more of in the future is virtual companies and human resources that would work closely together as employees, business partners, or contractors to realize projects or to create products and services. Unified communications is probably just at the beginning because the next step would be the merger of social networking and enterprise-ready unified communications. Perhaps we would just have to click on a "social contact" in our virtual address book in order to reach out to someone in the future. We may no longer require all contacts to be manually added or synchronized from one single database. Lync, Skype, and many other applications could bring this up to the next level where we communicate across technologies in our daily private and business life. No matter what technology we are using, we are able to search based on a skill or for a specific person across all social platforms and across many different unified communications and Collaborations technologies. We are then finally able to do what we originally wanted—simplifying the communication with people.

Unified communications connects people in a very efficient and fast way. You can "virtually" meet your team or customers to work on a Word or PowerPoint document together or use Lync to make phone calls. Real-time collaboration saves time, saves cost, and you have the whole world just a mouse click away.

The cost factor is especially important for unified communications projects. In the next chapter, we will learn more about the real cost saving factors and what a business case should contain for such projects.

5
Cost Optimization Approaches

In this chapter, we will focus our attention on how we can optimize cost. In the previous pages, I have described the impact of unified communications in many different areas and also the trend towards new social media and cloud technology in the market. One major reason why many unified communications or cloud projects are of such importance is their ability to bring about cost efficiency and cost savings. In this chapter we will talk about the key areas for cost saving, how to improve efficiency in the organization with simple examples, and how we can quantify these benefits.

Changes in recent years, especially during the post financial crisis years of 2009 and 2010, have brought about unprecedented challenges and risks. At the same time, these new conditions have created new opportunities for companies and employees today. This new competitive environment calls for effective, innovative, professional, and change-oriented management, from entrepreneurs to managers to specialists.

Need for an efficient communication solution

The turmoil caused by the collapse of the global financial system triggered uncertainties and had business impacts. In order to be prepared for new situations, a shift in priorities and realignment of resources are necessary. In today's world, the ability to react to situations is one behavior that few can afford to be without. When companies respond to changes in information and knowledge, they are forced to improve continuously, increasing efficiency, and ultimately surprising us. The demanding economic environment affects not only the companies locally but it has a global impact on the companies, which in turn triggers a global response.

In some cases, this means that the operating assets of a company are distributed worldwide, over resources, over the cost of the workforce, and production facilities. In other cases, through the use of the Internet, we are able to expand businesses into global markets, creating a competitive international business.

To obtain higher profits, achieve success, or be more competitive, many companies have supply chains and partnerships expanding all over the world. Due to new business conditions, the ability to optimize processes to support a global business system in order to be more efficient and economical is becoming one of the most important requirements for a technology manufacturer.

Another equally important factor is *security*. This is particularly relevant when you want your customers and partners to have confidence in your decisions for daily business and agreements. This is why many companies decide to use and store business information with different security as compared to the past.

These new uncertainties and challenges might seem intimidating at first glance. However, they should not deter you from making plans to change. Managers must consider their options carefully and work out an appropriate action plan which is based on their own strengths, financial situations, and needs of the enterprise. The output of the company's products and services would most likely have a significant impact on customers and users.

These economic conditions usually require the business processes to make adjustments to a certain extent. Undoubtedly, they will need to vigorously track their processes to reduce costs and allocate necessary resources for investments to create the potential for success. Investments can sometimes be neglected, especially in difficult times when there are simply no funds and the focus is simply on optimizing current potential.

The primary focus for IT managers is probably rapid reduction in costs. IT managers find ways to make structural changes in infrastructure and reduce operational support costs and the extent of supported services to provide long-term and sustainable savings for the company. Another possible solution is to optimize service cost centers that are needed for the work processes. The goal for companies is always to reduce cost and expenses; this is a common factor.

Economic pressure resulted in an overall tighter and smaller staff headcount with necessary restructuring and/or reduction in the number of employees in the company. Project expenses or budgets without clear strategic usages or short-term payback/amortization have to be justified by the management or put on hold.

Under these economic situations, the use of correct, truly sustainable, and cost-efficient IT communication solutions is a key success factor for optimizing in-house potential.

The use of unified communication solutions pays for itself as a cost reduction factor when companies are doing their annual budgeting, deciding on new investments or process improvements. The focus in the following pages of this chapter is on substantial savings and optimization opportunities that some large and medium-sized businesses can get when they have successfully implemented and utilized their unified communication solutions.

A Microsoft white paper, *Achieving Cost and Resource Savings with Unified Communications*, is used as supportive literature for the following information, content, and formulas used in the calculations.

In this book, you have learnt that thinking about unified communications includes having both mindset and technology changes in communication methods and platform solutions to increase efficiency.

Significant cutting-edge technologies have allowed companies to achieve immediate and lasting cost and resource savings. In the past, most business communication activities were mainly done by physically meeting up and speaking to business partners, through telephone calls that provide no facial information, or having business information written on paper and mailed to each other via postal mail or courier services. They were susceptible to delays and needed frequent workarounds. With unified communications, we are able to optimize communication by using software to support such activities to reduce costs and at the same time, achieve better results.

Optimization opportunities with UC

Unified communications provides significant opportunities for optimization in the following categories:

- Reduce the direct costs for communication services (for example, Internet and data connectivity, network location data lines, VoIP services, phone including landline and mobile bills, conference services such as audio and video conference hosting, and equipment) as well as associated expenses such as business travel.

- Optimization of communication infrastructure brings about a reduction in operating costs by replacing numerous diverse and decentralized old products with integrated features of a new UC solution. A well-known example is to optimize the old PBX/telecommunication infrastructure to potentially create cost savings for an organization or company.

- Promote individual and group productivity through cooperation and integration of knowledge management and collaboration, as UC is able to take advantage of the intellectual and human capital by providing professional management and secure communications, reducing unforeseen risks.

- Optimization of communication and collaboration workflows and process inside and outside the organization. An example is to improve the communication interface with customers and business partners in the form of "Federation" or even "Web RTC" (Web-based real-time communication) to engage customers with, for example sales or service support.

- Application development and extensibility on a unified communications platform is possible. Communication and collaboration features and key elements of a solution or platform can be extended using the company's resources and intellectual property as opposed to engaging a traditional PBX vendor/manufacturer to build an expensive extension into legacy systems.

- With unified communications in the cloud, the company is able to reduce the cost spent on hardware, hosting, maintenance, and update cycle. The company only needs to pay for all the real-time communication features that it uses.

Let us take a closer look at these optimization categories.

Reducing direct costs of communication services

The first step is to analyze the information and communication investments within the company. Very often companies give their budget for hosted conferencing services, fixed and mobile telephony, but not costs incurred and often they are not even aware of the details.

The most observable cost reduction opportunities are often found in the following areas:

Reducing the costs/fees for Internet and data services

Internet and data services are now considered an essential standard for information networks, information processing, and communication. If we were to take this opportunity to several companies and their providers asking about their data network models, we would find that more than two-thirds of their dedicated high-speed data lines with their providers are connected and have additional data packets to mobile phones. It is easier to network them, especially with modern network coverage like in Europe and Asia. A comparison of existing market telecommunication/Internet providers is an important step of analysis, since data packets and performance data on different carriers or provider networks have differing costs and can contribute to high costs. For many providers, it is not only about "the Internet cable" itself, but also includes the service scope and **Service Level Agreement (SLA)** as part of the entire package. This forces companies which are involved in optimization projects to make comparisons with other providers in the market.

Potential savings

It is important to do the homework and to identify and analyze the company's monthly data volume on data lines and then do the same for all mobile equipment. Determine what they are frequently used for, for example, surfing the Internet, checking e-mail/e-mail synchronization, share documents or other content, and so on.

The opportunity here is to compare with other providers. In practice, you should first speak to your current provider based on the data volume you are interested in and find out if there is a flat or optimized allocation cost model available in order to help save costs and increase efficiency. Sometimes it also makes sense to just renegotiate the agreement and get a better price rate or data plan for the entire organization or simply just for a small percentage of the employees. At the same time, you start looking at alternative providers and determine if they can offer you better service at a lower price.

The current usage of data services needs to be documented and historical reports of data volume and cost need to be prepared for detailed analysis when searching for a better service at a lower price. In the next stage, you move into optimization as a separate project.

Reducing costs/fees for conference services

Any company that engages external services for audio, video, or web conferencing has either lifetime contract payments or makes payments based on the number of users, offices, or even international subsidiaries. Instead of using an external "expensive" service or a hosted service with fixed costs and monthly/annual fee regardless of the number of external conference participants, with an appropriate choice of an internal conference system, service costs can be greatly reduced. This gives the company the ability to rapidly achieve cost optimization with a high ROI and a better **Total Cost of Ownership (TCO)**.

The highest savings come mostly from web conferencing (sharing desktops, presentations, documents, and applications) and video conferencing as such services are frequently calculated at a per minute rate and are additional costs.

Savings from audio conferencing is also possible when it is done internally. The per-minute prices for external audio conferencing, although essentially lower than those for video conferencing, are usually also paid more frequently. So an alternative for external service is a cost-effective internal audio conferencing service that needs to be implemented into the organization's own IT infrastructure. At the same time there should be an identification process to check if a cloud offering or a cloud service of the required infrastructure would be a possible option.

If there are no services for telephone or video conferences within the company but there are high costs due to high communication traffic, an investment in a communication system could result in cost optimization.

By targeting these communications, you may achieve a significant potential for savings when you drive a solid in-house service or also a *more cost efficient* cloud and hosted service.

Potential savings

Unified communications, as described in the previous chapters, significantly reduce the cost of your communications support.

This very effective solution contributes to the reduction or elimination of fees for outside services. The Lync Server is thus a leading "unified" conferencing solution which offers a complete set of voice, web, and video conferencing capabilities as well as unique features such as the integration of existing infrastructure or the option to use cost-efficient technology such as the Polycom CX5000 conference device for voice and video capabilities in conference rooms.

The system is also compatible with almost any standard webcam and even offers integration into existing systems such as those from Polycom, Hewlett-Packard, and Cisco Tandberg Systems. In addition to functioning as a video conferencing platform, Lync Server also provides the integration of a telephone conference service (Conference Bridge) coupled with your PBX or the telephone provider, to allow you to easily have telephone conferences with external/internal users through the system. In summary, these functions allow the acquisition and replacement of all corresponding external services. The total cost can therefore be reduced, using Lync as a server in both online and cloud services.

There are many well-known companies that have already adopted such solution sets. One of the world's best-known companies, Intel Cooperation (`www.Intel.com`) achieved 20 percent cost savings with the introduction of unified communications solely using audio conferencing. Other customer references can be found on the Microsoft Lync web page: `http://lync.microsoft.com`.

It is particularly important to highlight that internal audio and video conferences have rapid payback, usually within six to eight months. This is because many services for audio and video conferences are calculated per minute to provide flexibility in the amount used and have user fees from 150 to over 10,000 USD per month depending on the usage. The operating costs for internal online meeting conferences with Lync are well below the previously-mentioned average cost per user per month, and thus deploying Lync as a unified communications platform, whether on-premise or as hosted services, provides cost optimization by reducing costs and increasing efficiency.

For these reasons, the total cost savings often pays for a unified communications project after one quarter.

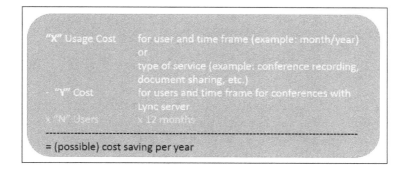

```
"X" Usage Cost      for user and time frame (example: month/year)
                    or
                    type of service (example: conference recording,
                    document sharing, etc.)
- "Y" Cost          for users and time frame for conferences with
                    Lync server
x "N" Users         x 12 months
-------------------------------------------------------------------
= (possible) cost saving per year
```

You can easily calculate how much you pay for your current service provider, and your telephone and video conferences by using the formula based on your user and usage.

Reducing costs/charges for mobile and fixed line telephony

For many companies, there is a considerable amount of scope that you can look into to reduce fees or costs for landline and mobile telephone calls. Although the cost of local calls and long distance calls has dropped significantly in recent years, the fees for international communications are still pretty high.

In most companies, the estimated bills for mobile telephony frequently come to several hundred dollars per month. International calls on mobile phones can cost much higher, especially if they have employees, customers, and partners in other countries. The use of a secure VoIP and communications solution can reduce phone calls to outside providers by having these calls transmitted over the data network of the company or the Internet. The cost of these calls is paid for by placing it into the cost of the communication networks, which can even be used to implement toll-free calls over the network.

The more relevant way of optimizing and reducing both fixed and mobile phone charges is to have and make use of presence information (availability information) to prevent unnecessary and unreachable calls to anyone, which can be especially useful on mobile devices.

In addition, instant messages can replace many short phone calls and may form a large part of communication. For all mobile phone calls in countries where the caller pays for the talks, a unified communications solution coupled with the telephone system of the company or a direct connection with the telecommunication service provider allows the mobile user (the initiator of the call) to contact the end user. Using the automated callback function from the unified communications system, they are able to make calls by connecting through the network/server in order to avoid fees on the mobile telephone network. Another option here is to initiate the call in the target country (local phone breakout).

This feature is known as "callback" or "single number reach" in telecommunications language.

Along with this "callback" function, Lync also offers the option to communicate through a pure VoIP connection between mobile clients. As the client communicates to another client using a mobile data connection, roaming costs or charges per minute would become obsolete. We will explain this in more detail in the following section.

Potential savings

Unified communications offers secure VoIP communication so the cost of your landline and mobile telephone calls can be reduced significantly.

The Lync Server provides a very easy way to communicate using a mouse click with users on a PC or a web browser connected with a VoIP device, such as VoIP phones, headsets, and handsets.

The Lync Server stands out here because it supports a large number of devices so it provides the maximum possibility to support any customer and business partner to have secure conversations, maximizing the opportunities for fee reductions.

For mobile phone users, the Lync Server provides a mobile client that can be used with the Windows Phone, RIM BlackBerry, Apple/iPhone, or Nokia, and which provides the ability to check the presence status of the person before the telephone call.

The solution provides availability of information or presence status, enables the user to set the call forwarding to a voicemail solution (for example, Exchange Server), or the writing of instant messages. In many cases, you can also use an instant message instead of calling to convey the message to the intended recipient.

With the previously-mentioned "callback" or "single number reach" functionality, users can place their own calls on the mobile phone, which initiates the Lync Server and automatically connects with the right person.

The Lync Server calls the mobile phone first and then establishes a session with the desired contact. The cost of this Lync voice call is, in this case, the same as a phone call through the local PBX system in the company. Particularly when abroad, this technology is important as roaming costs and mobile phone charges will be limited. Fees are also avoided, for example, when a traveler goes to distant land logs on the Internet and uses the Lync Server to make the VoIP connections. He or she would be able to speak or make local calls through the Lync Server free of charge with their colleagues in the office.

However, using the previously-mentioned savings through unified communications to generate a sustainable added value requires, first and foremost, an analysis of the mobile and fixed line telephony costs. There is also another option to select a mobile or telecommunication service provider which offers a flat fee for international calls from the company's cell phones and for the office phones in the company.

As mentioned earlier, Lync 2013 mobile clients have the ability to allow a Lync mobile client to communicate with another Lync mobile client through the data connection only. Lync 2013 also offers the extension to video calls next to the VoIP audio calls. The great advantage here is that user A could call user B from any location in the world through a wireless connection or data connection — for example, **Universal Mobile Telecommunications Systems (UMTS)** — for audio calls, video calls, and online meetings. Another example would be that companies who are federated with each other can use the same feature for mobile communications or to join online meetings without additional costs for roaming through the mobile carrier. The same feature can be used if Skype mobile (Skype mobile to Skype mobile calls) is installed on the Windows Phone, IPhone, Blackberry, or Android device. Microsoft is also working on the communication capabilities between Skype and Lync for mobile devices with the extension of the Lync and Skype Federation.

Going back to the traditional phone call, the extent of international or local telephone call usage is a relevant factor for the cost calculation. If all costs made were recorded in a preliminary analysis (assessment) and there were high communication costs and call charges in the company, we can estimate the payback would be in just a few months. If Lync to Lync/Skype calls are used on the mobile device it would be important to calculate the cost reduction up to 100 percent, and only calculate the cost for data connection for the mobile extension or device.

"X" Communication cost per month − 70* percent cost reduction
+ "Y" average of mobile usage per month
x 12 months x "N" users

= (possible) cost saving per year

*= estimation for potential cost reduction

Optimizing communication and collaboration cost by using Federation

From Office Communications Server 2007, Microsoft introduced the ability to "federate" with other organizations that are also using a Microsoft unified communications platform. The best way for an organization to use Federation is to add contacts and people groups from other organizations to their own contact list in the Lync client. Of course, in terms of security, it would be possible to restrict the ability to add others outside the organization and also what kind of communication capabilities are enabled between any two organizations. The term federation is also used when Lync-enabled users in a company invite other users outside the organization for a chat or audio conversation who are using other services such as Skype and Yahoo Messenger. Either way, federation is a great opportunity to reduce costs of telecommunication by reducing the telephony bill. Big organizations including Microsoft, HP, Polycom, and many others that are using Lync or OCS have allowed federation to customers and business partners to increase the level of efficiency and to reduce the cost for telecommunication.

The math for this is quite simple; instead of making phone calls through the landline, cell phone, or the configured voice extension on the Lync server/client, a user in company A calls a user in company B through the Lync client. Even if the other side is using another technology like for example Skype, conversation by audio and chat (in future also video with most of the other services) is possible. Microsoft is actively engaged in reducing the high telephony bill by more than 50 percent with federation technology and they are still trying to improve for more cost saving. With federation, it is also possible to optimize cost for very special business areas in the company or in outsourced divisions. For contact centers or call centers, it would be, for example, possible to use federation between business partners that are part of the support process. Let us use Microsoft as an example; Microsoft are in "federation" with some of their outsourced contact centers, and they are able to communicate practically with no cost on the telephony side. This concept could be developed further to include customers who use "federation" or VoIP technology to connect to customer support or to a customer representative in a sales division by VoIP service via Skype, or even a web page per Web RTC and callback solutions.

Reducing costs/fees for equipment setting up

Another factor in reducing cost is in reducing the running cost of the equipment. The cost of facilities, including rental payments, office furniture, and operating costs such as lighting, heating, electricity, water, and security have important potential for reduction. Many companies use unified communications solutions to allow employees to work outside the office or be mobile so they are able to work from home part time.

Mobile working or so-called "home office culture" may not always be possible to implement in all forms of enterprise; since all businesses are different, this is a question which every company needs to answer for themselves. It is important to highlight that there have been many studies on homeworking or remote working, which have mostly demonstrated increased productivity and satisfaction levels in employees. At the same time, there are many organizations or companies that are uncomfortable about their employees working outside the company's compounds because they cannot track their productivity. The last few years have shown that this is a rapidly changing factor because mobile or remote working has become more and more common and could be one of the main working models in the near future.

By analyzing employees in companies, studies have also shown that longer commuting times decrease both employee satisfaction and productivity, but these measures increase if they have efficient technology made available for them to work from anywhere—both inside and outside the company.

Once these programs are introduced and regulated by the companies' "working" policies, savings can be achieved by the remaining internal staff. Light, electricity, heating, and other operating costs for all areas, floors, or buildings can be shut down or better regulated. Of course, new technologies in the facility can also help to reduce cost. Many companies have already begun reducing in-house facilities based on the assumption that a certain percentage of employees would work remotely, in order to optimize their spending. Microsoft Switzerland is a good example here. This Microsoft subsidiary reduced the number of working units at the office so that it only need to provide work spaces for 60 percent to 80 percent of their staff. The rest of their staff is constantly busy with customers and business partners outside the company or works from home. Similarly, Microsoft Austria has also made the same decision and implemented the "workplace of the future" with mobile desks and office space for only around 40 percent of their staff; their savings are estimated to be millions of dollars per year.

Potential savings

Unified communications is suitable and ideal for flexible workplace design. The Lync Server and Exchange Server also offer a variety of communication and collaboration capabilities such as voicemail, mobile e-mail, instant messaging, text to speech, speech to text, voice, audio or video conferences, and much more.

The Microsoft SharePoint Server, SkyDrive, and SkyDrive Professional also allow the storage and use of documents, forms, and other data from anywhere in the world, without **Virtual Private Network** (**VPN**) technology and without security concerns. Staff can have access anytime and from any location to the complete unified communications and collaborations system and they are able to work more efficiently and from any location and time zone.

With availability information, your employees can easily share information and have real-time communication with the team, your customers, and partners. This technology also allows saving, for example in the need to have fully equipped workstations and a reduction in the number of monitors, chairs, tables, telephones, meeting rooms, and much more, because employees need to be provided only with sufficient work equipment (such as a notebook, headset, mobile phone, tablet PC, and so on) to carry out their work. Unified communications in the form of Persistent Chat also offers a great way to dramatically reduce the communication and collaboration costs between several different users, both inside and outside the organization. We have already come across the term Persistent Chat in earlier chapters. The ability to create managed chat rooms and to invite specific people and groups into these rooms can save the time required to resolve a specific problem in the workflow of a project or a customer case. Persistent Chat is another way in which companies such as banks, technology providers, service providers, system integrators, and other vertical businesses can optimize their time and cost required for communication. The business case here is to enable groups to resolve a topic faster without having the need to set up conference calls and to be constantly available at the same time—persistent communication and collaboration.

Optimizing travel expenses and business travel

Travel expenses are another form of expenditure and that can use unified communications as an important communications-based savings opportunity. You can achieve an immediate reduction of current expenditure by restricting business travel of employees. However, this does not mean that the effectiveness of the company is reduced. Audio, web, and video conferencing solutions provided by unified communications can more than ensure the effectiveness of the company is maintained. With recording options and the possibility of keeping meeting content stored in shared workspaces, team members can stay informed about the meetings that they are unable to participate in.

The expansion of business functions for conferences with partners and customers was described in detail in *Chapter 3, Business Cooperation in the World of the World Wide Web*. Joint ventures in the world of Web 2.0 allow us to have larger savings potential.

Potential savings

Whether the Lync Conference technology is hosted on the server or as an online version (cloud services, Office 365), it's an excellent tool for achieving these savings targets. The Lync Server has a common document working function enabled whether you have planned a telephone or video conference with customers and partners. Unified communications enables many variants of use to provide a high degree of support for businesses. Rather than backing out of meetings or presentations that are far away, they can still make their presentation by scheduling an ad hoc video conference, with high quality audio and video with a single click launched from the Outlook Calendar. Some companies go one step further and calculate a more intensive investment base exchange for implementing the unified communications technology, which would create situations that would not otherwise have been possible.

What does this mean? It's simple. Instead of making two appointments with clients in a day, employees can have a lot more meetings due to not being interrupted by the journey to and from the meetings. Employees can easily have the meeting anywhere and anytime. Naturally, face-to-face personal contact can never be fully replaced. However, it is unnecessary to be personally present on site for every meeting and presentation. For example, Microsoft Corporation's quarterly and budget planning can be done through video conferencing and you only need to make business travel to the headquarters in Redmond, Washington, United States for important meetings and events.

If an analysis of travel expenses within your company by the finance or business leadership department is available, this is the best basis for evaluating potential savings. Based on these data average travel costs per employee or business and using the following formula the ROI, can be calculated and then optimized:

```
"X" Percentage of all "traveling" employees
x "X" Business travels per day/month/year and every employee
x "X" Cost per business travel
x "X" Percentage of reduction (example: 2 travels per year)
-------------------------------------------------------------
= (possible) cost saving per year
```

The next section goes more into the details of "optimization of communications infrastructure". For example, the messaging system used in the company, the management and administrative expenses and fees for service contracts, with optimizations in language systems, servers, and sites.

Optimizing communication infrastructure and replacing legacy technology

The integration of various communication options such as instant messaging, e-mail, voicemail, resource management, data storage, audio, video, and web conferencing in a simple, unified communications solution is a major potential for savings. Another way to optimize the communication infrastructure would be to look into replacing old legacy technologies such as old PBX systems with unified communications. There are various different UC solutions on the market that are all great ways to replace the old systems with the new. Legacy systems are usually expensive to maintain, or less extensible and need a lot of traditional telecommunication engineers or business partners to maintain. Many organizations are therefore engaged in replacing these systems with the new unified communications platforms.

Based on personal experience in this space, it makes sense to compare all required functions from the legacy system with the replacement choice of UC solutions and platforms before moving forward with the change. This is especially important because some scenarios and features might require additional software-based solutions on the top of the UC platform. It might be necessary to invest additionally in software development projects depending on the business requirements. Using Lync as an example, additional developments would be necessary for the integration of an automatic door opening system for the main entrance in the company or to have the integration of a customer care solution extended with speech recognition into Lync. Another factor is that many companies are very cautious and they find it difficult to trust a software-based solution that can handle all communications to customers and business partners. In all replacement projects, there must be a detailed design and planning process as well as good project management to deliver a UC-only solution as the overall telecommunication. The successes of these projects have brought about a significant cost reduction in many different areas.

Another important factor as mentioned in the beginning is that many companies can now have a single application and technology for various components such as audio conferencing, video conferencing, and so on. These technology areas that were usually several separate systems now have standard interfaces that can "talk" to one another, so the user can have a functional IT and telecommunication system.

An extension or telephone system at each company's site is frequently accompanied by a related voicemail, **interactive voice response (IVR)** systems, call centers, and one console for call accounting and administration. In most companies using unified communications, this is a combination of systems using one or just a few applications that are easier to handle and to maintain. If a company also has other subsidiaries, in other words "sites", it is important that a unified communications platform like Lync is able to consolidate all communication resources and decentralize them to the other subsidiaries. For example, international companies can have x number of Lync pools to handle all communication and collaboration capabilities instead of having a PBX solution in every subsidiary. This means that other remote offices and subsidiaries of this organization have a secure connection to the central unified communications platform that would enable them to stay connected and to communicate in a highly secure manner.

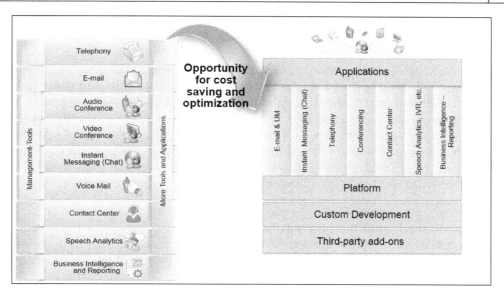

Potential savings

This saving measure can be implemented more frequently in the short term, since many PBXs and voicemail systems were installed at the end of the 90s and manufacturer support lasts a long time. Decisions must be made in such cases. The decision to apply the consolidation model usually leads to big savings and sustainable optimization. The procedure is to provide a central platform to replace the current legacy solution or to expand the existing equipment. The Lync Server and Exchange Server have the technical solution models for the different locations to be brought together and then gradually put them on the central platform to be turned on. Also, the cloud version of Lync and especially Exchange can help to outsource specific services and to reduce cost to a minimum within a short amount of time. Although some special elements such as IVR or complex call center solutions can probably not be included, the majority of the legacy systems can be integrated in a very easy way to achieve a high ROI.

Both products have a very functional platform for the consolidation of systems, from voice communications to e-mail or management of mobile devices. Voicemail, text messaging, communication journals, business intelligence, reporting, the integration of mobile devices, and the IVR functionality are integrated into the Exchange Server and Lync, Lync **Response Group Services** (**RGS**), and real-time communications such as instant messaging, video and audio conferencing, desktop sharing, online meeting are part of the Lync Server.

In addition, the management of the systems plays an essential role in reducing accumulating costs and ongoing operating costs. A very interesting example is the RGS, which offers the automation of call workflows based on the presence information to other users inside the organization. Many customers use RGS services and IVR based on Lync in customer facing communications in order to reduce the cost required to find the right and available person. RGS is of course not a full contact center solution for Lync but it can help in many cases to optimize certain communication workflows for customers and business partners. Lync also offers server-side **Application Program Interfaces (API)**, which provide the ability to extend RGS and IVR functionalities to be used in contact center deployments for Lync in many different scenarios to reduce cost or to gain more efficiency.

Since the Lync Server and Exchange Server software are integrated software environments, each with their own management interface, there is a considerable saving potential with administration. Lync Server and Exchange Server, in terms of their flexibility in supporting groups, geographic regions, and mobile workers (sales, technical, support staff, and so on) are remarkable.

The realization of a unified communications project helps to avoid costs that become immediately noticeable and quickly identify savings from the ongoing cost of maintenance contracts for old PBX lease and voicemail systems. Therefore, begin with divisions or locations where such a project has the largest (and most rapid) influence in order to provide you with so-called quick wins. However, do not forget internal communication of project successes, or support of the project promoters or of the external project partners to the management.

Advantages of cloud services

Cloud technology and services is one of the major topics in current business. Cloud technology offers many ways to outsource standard services such as e-mail, storage, physical hardware, and other types of IT areas more cost efficiently into cloud services. Communication and collaboration services are great business areas to consider if having them as cloud services would offer any financial and functional benefit to the company.

Either way, it is important to work on a baseline of current equipment such as hardware (servers and so on), software that is used for several different areas of business scenarios, development approach (for example, customized unified communications based applications), operational and maintenance workload, and of course storage and other types of current investments in information and communication technology and equipment.

The business case for cloud services is not only thinking in terms of having more or less outsourced business applications and hardware. The cloud also offers benefits such as having lower energy cost or storage cost for server farms that are required in mid to large companies. When the cost of hardware decreases, the proportion of energy cost for servers and equipment increases and this may add up to 20 to 30 percent of the total cost for already energy efficient server hardware, network equipment, and cooling systems (air conditions for server rooms). With more development of the cloud services, we might see a future where datacenters are commonly outsourced and available in the cloud for businesses. Standard IT services are also available as relatively inexpensive hosted services; IT maintenance and telecommunication technology are commonly used and purchased as a cloud service.

However, there are several different types of cloud, such as a private cloud or public cloud in the current repertoire of services available. Private cloud environments are beneficial for companies which require a certain level of compliance or customization that public cloud services might not offer. Public cloud services are the most common cloud services where companies can purchase all kinds of business services with a *common* set of available security and compliance offerings. A good example of a public cloud is Microsoft's Office 365 standard offering. Of course Microsoft, just like other providers, also offers customized offerings for private cloud integration for almost all collaboration and communication as well as storage services. Even Office 365 can be combined with a customized installation of private cloud equipment and can be used for any sized companies with specific business requirements.

The section for cloud services in this chapter is just a very short summary of all deployment options, usage scenarios, and opportunities. There are also important design and planning considerations when a company is evaluating to use cloud technology for their business. As we are talking about a very specific part of the cloud area—the communication and collaboration area, it is important to be aware that traditional telecommunication and legacy technologies are targets for hosted services in the cloud. Microsoft, Cisco, IBM, Google, Avaya, and many other companies are offering different ways to bring the telecommunication equipment of customers to the next stage. Unified communications by Microsoft, in other words Lync, is part of the Office 365 offering and can be integrated as a cloud-only solution, in private cloud environments or in hybrid environments which are a mix of existing equipment (like integration with current PBX solution). The cloud has the same advantage, that the UC features are hosted in the cloud. The cost saving factor or simply the ROI is that the whole UC architecture, including the integration to a telecommunication services provider, can be placed in the cloud.

Users in the company need to connect only using a client (or softphone) application to the cloud service in order to use all of the offered communication and collaboration features. Of course, the selection of the cloud services provider is in itself a very important topic. How do you determine the *best*, *most reliable*, and *most economic* cloud services provider. The choice of provider in part also determines the overall cost saving factor. However, it is also important that the technology offered by the provider has all the required features so that you are able to make a comparison on the different types of unified communication deployments and to make the decision on whether to deploy this in a cloud or not.

To consider cloud services in the right way, it is important to calculate the ROI in terms of current cost for IT and telecommunication equipment, available unified communications and collaboration services in the current or future deployment, license cost, energy, other infrastructure cost, maintenance, support cost, and the required human resources to manage everything. In many scenarios, it makes sense to use unified communications services as a cloud service, especially for small and medium sized companies that have not had a unified communications solution implemented before. For more complex or larger companies, it is usually the case to have a mix of cloud services and hybrid deployment or to use only a part of the unified communications and collaborations technology in the cloud and the rest on site. A good example would be to use Lync online for chat, audio, and video communication but SharePoint and Exchange as cloud services.

Whatever the best solution might be for your organization, there are many areas to consider and it is a must-have action item to have a detailed business plan for the financials and also to consider the technological impact on the company when a cloud service or an on-site integration is implemented.

Optimization of existing infrastructure

Let us come back from the cloud discussion into the common areas of IT and telecommunication infrastructure. The combination of communication services in the company as mentioned is a possible first step for optimizing costs. However, we find that in most companies, we have the other frequently mentioned cost drivers. This technique now gives us the possibility of using existing infrastructure without loss of function to integrate into new and more efficient, and ultimately more effective solutions.

A variant would be the use of 64-bit servers and virtual servers and if possible, merging the servers of the corporate offices or departments; at the same time, bear in mind that they are required to maintain separate identities or domains. It is important to highlight that 64-bit servers are already a common standard but many companies are still using 32-bit applications and operation systems on it, which reduces the value and ROI of the hardware equipment.

Sharing 64-bit server hardware for several different business applications and usage scenarios and forcing a centralized consolidation reduces the cost of equipment and also supports remote locations. Another option is to consider optimization in the type of storage technology that gets used in the IT department. One example would be the elimination or avoidance of **Storage Area Network (SAN)** and **Network Attached Storage (NAS)** configurations in situations where there is a strong demand for expensive local or redundant systems for message storage or archiving. There is also a trend for **Direct Attached Storage (DAS)** solutions or technologies, which offer to use less expensive hardware with almost the same level of performance as expensive equipment (an example is Flash Disk technology). Microsoft Exchange is a good example which is able to use inexpensive DAS storage systems to store a mailbox and configuration data of the mail system. Of course it is also important to mention here again the cloud technology at this point. The cloud offers a high ROI in scenarios where data can be stored in an outsourced cloud datacenter, which we described in the previous section.

Next is the summary of important messaging-based applications and proprietary applications. This is a frequent series of independent local systems for compatibility, archiving, control of spam and viruses, allowing messaging-based workflow applications, supporting shared folders, and even voice-messaging.

In many cases, these locally distributed applications will be merged to reduce enormous costs in operation and maintenance.

Potential savings

To summarize, this frequently mentioned saving can be implemented in the short term if the following cost drivers are optimized:

- Reduce the number of serviceable and supporting servers.
- Consolidation of server applications into virtual environments or into more powerful shared server equipment (if the application supports applications such as SharePoint and Archiving applications on the same server hardware).
- Consolidation or elimination of the extension of additional SAN-/NAS-System for storage and archiving.

- Automation of the e-mail server deployment and administration management.
- Consolidation of migration or security applications such as anti-spam and anti-virus applications to a unified solution in the company or consideration of cloud and hosted services.

Optimization of software licenses

In the previous chapters, you have already read several savings optimizations that unified communications bring. In any case, an important issue to remember at this point is the possibility of optimization by means of a suitable software licensing program or in other words the type of licensing for the unified communication platform within the company.

One need is to identify existing license agreements and to negotiate, purchase, and renew orders and license agreements in the most efficient way. Users or application licenses can be changed with mostly no or little cost compared to antiquated license programs and agreements. Cost savings are also possible because performance requirements for new businesses can be met with unified communications or related applications that are bundled in license packages.

It is important to generally look at all departments, IT, telecommunications, and facilities management, including business areas, and question where the software packages are used and also how they are licensed. When in discussion with the purchasing departments and their procurement, it is important to question them about the licensing and to obtain the information and dates of existing contracts.

Potential savings

In terms of the Microsoft unified communications solution, there are many ways to license everything correctly and effectively. The base license option offers instant messaging, presence integration, or audio/video communication (Standard Client Access License), the "Enterprise" option offers video conferencing (one:many and many:many conferencing), and the "Plus or Voice" option enables voice communication per PBX implementation or pure VoIP to a telecommunication services provider or carrier. More information can be found on the Microsoft License website at http://www.microsoft.com/calsuites.

Take advantage of knowledge and human capital

The main focus when it comes to knowledge and human capital is to enable real productivity gains in business areas because resources and knowledge within the company have to achieve business goals which are aligned to the livelihood of the company.

Human efficiency in organizations with important issues and existing findings is probably one of the most controversial topics and would fill far more than a chapter in a book. In this section, we will, however, specifically look at the possibilities in terms of efficiency of the staff and the principle of "cooperation" in the company.

This can be done at two different levels:

- General staff efficiency
- Improved workgroup processes and collaborative projects

In addition, organizations should take precautions to avoid costly incidents due to data leaks and the failure to meet regulatory and legal requirements. Using unified communications solutions, the employee needs to have secure communication and management needs to be compliant in terms of data protection and privacy. On this subject there is an "Operating Agreement" document draft (without any legal guarantee) in the appendix of this book, which offers a template for a potential discussion about compliance and security in the own company and organization.

Potential savings

The improvement of the staff efficiency may be significantly critical in terms of the overall efficiency output of the organization. With unified communication solutions, the opportunity exists to eliminate communication-related barriers in everyday work environments.

Among the most important savings are tools for presence and instant messaging so that the right resources can be immediately found, and phone calls and messages for people who are unavailable can be avoided. Additional savings come from simplified communication tasks, such as communicating via a mouse click from a document, e-mail, or a contact name. The next step is to allow access from anywhere so that users can be productive on the road, which helps to save time while traveling. This means we can have fewer people handling the same job, resulting in savings for the department and ultimately at the enterprise level.

Market research firm Gartner and Forrester Research presented studies estimating that 10 minutes to 60 minutes of increased productivity in each individual employee per day equates to savings of 2 percent to 12 percent of overall working time. To achieve these savings, departments facing situational hiring freezes, overtime cuts, or layoffs should react by providing new IT/Telecommunications unified communications tools (and training) for the remaining employees.

Rapid deployment of these new tools is particularly important for areas with customer contact, such as sales, customer service, and customer care. To achieve optimal productivity of employees in communication, the ideal solution is to enable Unified collaboration using the Microsoft suite of communications solutions—the Lync Server, Exchange Server, as well as the SharePoint Server.

To achieve these productivity gains to the fullest extent, Microsoft's unified communications solution also offer access from anywhere via PC, laptop, tablet PC, mobile device, web browser, and other line of business applications.

Microsoft Unified Communications uses Microsoft Office to provide sustainable efficiency. The ability to integrate and expand the Microsoft Unified Communications platform into customized enterprise solutions helps to reduce the cost of technology needed to achieve the required enterprise communication for the businesses, hence reducing the information cost within the organization. Another last important term is "federation". With the option to federate different companies to each other, it is possible to expand the cost saving and efficiency factors not only inside the organization, but across all business partners or customers and to achieve a greater saving or efficiency factor in a more global economical way.

Business value assessment

Making an assessment of the potential ROI of unified communications in your own company or in a customer organization is usually a very complex procedure. Many areas need to be analyzed, compared, and calculated in terms of the financial opportunities when moving into the new world of communications and collaborations. The previously listed areas help to recognize some of the major areas to reduce costs with UC or to increase efficiency for employees and the organization. Microsoft offers business partners and customers a great guide on how to drive sales and deployments for Lync and in future, also Skype business opportunities on the MS partner website at `https://mspartner.microsoft.com/en/us/pages/solutions/lync-accelerate.aspx`.

Microsoft offers documentation, and video/web casts to help you prepare for UC projects. Hardware and device catalogs for video conference devices, headsets and other devices, Lync bandwidth calculators, and lots of other helpful content and tools are available as well. I would like to highlight the Lync Business Value Assessment tool. This helps customers and partners to analyze important areas (as mentioned before) for Lync and unified communications projects, and how this might affect the TCO and ROI.

Another website I would recommend reading is the "Lync Accelerate" website. It should be read before embarking on any kind of unified communications project and should be used as part of the overall planning and design process as well.

Summary

Every IT infrastructure or telecommunication services project in the face of major changes needs to have a very strong business case. Companies who have integrated unified communications successfully in their organization achieved a real cost saving or satisfaction factor through better communication tools, better interfaces for customers, and so on. They had gone through detailed planning and addressed all the key areas of the existing environment. For some organizations, these are savings from non-major business travel through the use of video conferencing; other companies implemented UC to have a faster and more cost-efficient communication workflow with their customers. It is very important to do your homework based on the key areas that are important for your organization, and go through each cost saving or efficiency factor to build a strong business justification and case for your project proposal, which eventually needs to be approved by the stakeholders and management.

We are about to move on to a very important chapter; it is now time to see what a real project would look like. The next chapter covers a real but anonymous project where unified communications and Lync were realized.

6
Unified Communications Projects in Practice

In this chapter, we will go through the creation of a practical customer project.

The objective of this chapter is to use a common project scenario to demonstrate how traditional telephony can be integrated into a new software-based communication technology, especially where desktop PCs and the physical network environment needs to be a part of the change and project scope.

By using a fictional company called Contoso, we will see how the Microsoft Unified Communications platform is implemented based on very specific business requirements in an enterprise.

Other than learning how to evaluate, drive, and realize unified communications projects, there are also a number of other important takeaway points in this chapter. It includes preparation/work that needs to be done in order to convince all your stakeholders to support the project, and the change in the collaboration and communication both inside and outside the company.

Even if you have a good business case, you would face tons of obstacles that could prevent this innovative technology from replacing the traditional telecommunication and information technology division in your company.

At the end of this chapter, you will find a checklist of the most important topics as a reference for preparation of a UC project. For a better overview, here are the stages that we will cover in this chapter:

Initial situation

Contoso is a medium-sized insurance company with around 5,000 employees operating from the main business area in Seattle. It has about 2,000 people who are field service insurance agents and are stationed outside their main company at 20 general agencies in Seattle, each with about 10 employees. The company planned to perform a nationwide Windows XP to Windows 8 Upgrade for all PC workstations at the end of the year.

All employees have an MS Exchange e-mail account (On-Premise version) and enterprise Office Professional license. The insurance software that allows range calculations and claims regulations is Citrix based and runs as a terminal server application in the enterprise environment.

For telephony, the customer has a Siemens HiPath 4000 PBX system located in the main office and several small telephone systems from different manufacturers in the general agencies. From the network point of view, the general agencies are connected via a redundant **Multi Protocol Label Switching** (**MPLS**) network to the main office. There was no specific reason, be it the expiry of a lease agreement for the PABX/ PBX location or a business acquisition, for the company to even consider the topic of UC. However, the financial crisis and its consequences forced the board to look for new opportunities for cost savings. A specialist in the field of UC consulting offered to analyze the effects of the introduction of a UC solution to the company and the remuneration of the consultant would be a part of the demonstrable savings, through the implementation of the proposals.

The role of a UC solution

A UC solution must enable the communication and collaboration of people who are at separate locations. This is necessary because many companies, increasingly, require mobility for employees, so effective communication and collaboration must also be able to take place outside the office environment. Another reason for this mobility is to create a better or more flexible work environment in the company. Many organizations change their model so as to allow home office for certain business areas or divisions. Many international studies show that by allowing information workers to work from anywhere, anytime (which includes working from home) increases the efficiency of an organization. If your organization is considering this step, you would also need to think about the company policy for mobile working. An organization needs to "trust" that their workers are doing their work even when they are off-site. Policies in the organization should also ensure that the employees have the right to disconnect from work after work hours and be able to have a good work/life balance.

Another aspect to consider, in the "choice" of the right solution for Contoso, is to analyze their communication and collaboration strategy. Even without talking about features and functions, it is very important to question how the company wants to communicate and collaborate with their customers and business partners and how the headquarter communicates/collaborates with their several subsidiaries. It is important to find out how the current communication strategy looks like before and assess it carefully even before talking about the new features. This additional knowledge could be used in the evaluation process for the right technical solution. Many years ago, companies derived their telecommunication approach, e-mail, meetings, video conferencing structure (mostly just for executives), and other communication strategy in a relative manner, based on cost savings and optimization opportunities alone. Contoso is an example of a relatively innovative company which is interested in major improvements and has the ability to execute a technology change. For larger organizations, it is extremely important to think how they can merge or change from their legacy equipment and technology to a more efficient way of communication and collaboration which is known as unified communications.

Since we are talking about new ways of communication, having a unified communications strategy which includes a mobile and social networking strategy inside the organization is an absolute must. Well-known research institutes forecast the choice of communication technology and interfaces and how communication and collaboration when realized within a company's ecosystem would determine how successful they are in the industry and in their vertical business.

Trends of communications in the Modern Office
(source: http://www.microsoft.com/en-us/news/features/2012/sep12/09-24Exchange.aspx)

Therefore, a good UC solution should have the following areas included:

- An integration of all communication and collaboration modalities (such as instant messaging, video, or telephony) so that the solution is easy to use and is accepted by employees.

- A location-independent access to all communication media, thus the use of the solution can be done in the same way from the office, from home, and from a mobile device (hotel hotspot).

- Integration of the communication media in standard business applications, **Line of Business** (**LOB**) applications, so that the operation can be effectively supported by the solution. For example, integrate **Customer Relationship Management** (**CRM**) software and customer care applications. Create custom development of applications inside the company. Integrate with mobile and other applications. This also means an investment in custom development because such integration is usually not part of an out of the box UC platform/solution. However, it is important to have the ability to connect line of business applications with a UC platform and by doing so real value is generated for the business.

- Integration of status indicators (presence integration) for efficient connectivity among all end users and also devices.

- A company-wide operation as multimedia collaboration today, and not just between employees of the same company, but also with employees of partner companies and their customers.

- The ability to choose UC as a cloud service or an on-premise service. If this is not available at the point of time the decision for a specific solution is being made, at least a possible migration or way for UC to coexist as a cloud service should be offered in a mid- or long-term roadmap. This is important for further cost optimization opportunities and also acts as a technology roadmap for communication and collaboration platforms.

- The ability to integrate UC, or at least certain UC capabilities, as a web application. In other words, is Web **Real Time Communication/Collaboration** (**RTC**) integrated natively in the browser technology or is web-enabled RTC (be able to be used as an UC add-on in the browser for communication) on the roadmap for this UC platform? This is important to leverage interfaces for better communication with customers and business partners and to be able to set up specific communication-enabled workflows among all communication parties.

For more information on Web RTC go to `http://www.webrtc.org/;` `http://en.wikipedia.org/wiki/WebRTC.`

Even for industry experts, it is difficult to have an overview and be up to date with all the available UC solutions in the market. All known solutions such as telephone systems (PBX) have recently, through software version upgrades, mutated in a wonderful manner without redesign into multimedia communication platforms. Such new products have raised the competition in the UC solutions market; UC solutions now find themselves in a market that is an intersection between telephony, unified messaging, and other forms of new communication like voice and web conferencing systems, e-mail solutions, and document management systems. Future development roadmaps show closer integration and extension to social networks such as Facebook, Microsoft Yammer, Linkedin, XING, and many others.

Every year Gartner, the market research and consulting company, publishes a magic quadrant that illustrates the development and growth of unified communications and other technologies (such as social networks, mobility, cloud technology, and so on) for businesses. From 2010 to 2013, the Gartner magic quadrant has shown a change in priority for the technologies it presents to customers and what is offered in communication and collaboration capabilities in UC platforms. The integration of unified communications, cloud services, and social networks seems to be a trend for the next couple of years. More information can be accessed at the Gartner website.

The preceding graphic shows the trending topics of 2013. You can see more at the Gartner website, `http://www.gartner.com/technology/home.jsp`.

However, a UC solution completely breaks the traditional market segments in the communications market. Each component of the UC solution comes from at least one of the specialized segments listed previously, has clear strengths in their niche market, and is at a different evolutional stage compared to other competitive solutions. Based on this, each of these components come together to form a complete UC solution. The UC solutions in the market comes in categories such as UC solutions with e-mail history, UC solutions with telephony, and UC solutions with hosting history. To find the optimal UC solution for a company, one must first focus on the right category within the UC market, the origin of which coincides with the most fundamental needs of the company.

In the case of Contoso, because of the distributed structure of the company and its communication behavior, their partners and clients have established e-mail as a primary means of communication so they should target a UC solution with strength in the e-mail field.

Evaluating UC solutions

After having a good overview on available solutions and technologies for real-time communication in the market, it is important to formulate the business requirements into a **Request for Proposal** (**RFP**) and address several different manufacturers for UC in the market. Although a RFP procedure should be "neutral", it is still important to limit the list of UC offerings during this process. A good number of "UC" manufacturers and offerings to have is around 10 to 15 depending on the complexity of the business requirements. The next concern is how the RFP is structured and what should be achieved by the RFP.

It is not only important to query the most important functionalities such as presence integration, instant messaging, telephony, teleconferencing, video conferencing, voicemail, fax, e-mail, web conferencing, desktop sharing, Web RTC, or the ability to extend to line of business applications but you must also assess how easy the functionalities would be for the majority of the staff to pick up and start using. The "ease of use", in other words the usability and user interface of the varied functions in a UC solution is of paramount importance, otherwise the solution will not be accepted by the employees and the increased efficiency and savings potential will not be realized. The worst scenario a company can face after the introduction of a UC solution is when the solution is running live but all the employees avoid using it.

One way to assess the usability of a UC solution is to weigh individual functionalities of the solution by a usability factor. The usability factor indicates how many steps (keystrokes, mouse clicks, and so on) must be performed by an employee to use the desired functionality and on how many different devices and mobile platforms the UC solution is available and if all required communication and collaboration modalities are available. The fewer the steps, the easier the operation, the higher the likelihood that employees will accept the proposed functionalities.

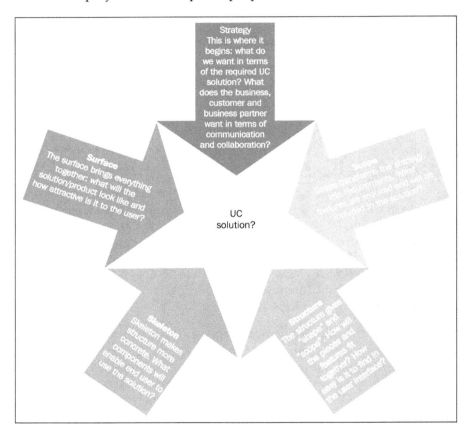

The preceding figure shows the important questions to check for usability. This decision framework can be used to analyze the "best fit" for the end users in the upcoming UC solution for the organization.

After evaluating the RFP document submitted by the different companies, Contoso awarded the UC solution from Microsoft as the solution that best fits the business requirements and the current installed base of Microsoft software on the PC workstations. This is due to the high usability factor as it has the typical "look and feel" of Microsoft products which leads to a high user acceptance.

Along with the RFP process of evaluating an available solution, it is also important to generate surveys with all the important key questions for employees in the different business areas. In other words, ask your sales department, business development areas, technical, IT, telecommunication, and of course the management. Everyone needs to be onboard for this upcoming project and a survey can help to identify additional key areas that you might have overlooked in the RFP or the front part research process.

In this example, the Contoso project team also asked different user groups and evaluated their answers together with the RFP to prepare the next steps for their UC project.

The Microsoft UC solution for Contoso

Based on the company's business requirements for a unified communications solution, Microsoft Lync stood out as it was able to offer key features and integration possibilities in the IT environment. The business requirements contain functional requirements, options to extend the UC solution into different areas such as contact center or custom development for web presence, and also the ability to replace certain parts of the legacy environment natively with a UC platform in the future. The selection process of the "right" UC solution was made by the procurement team of Contoso and the results were communicated back to the project team.

The following key features were the baseline for the decision to choose Lync:

- Mature presence platform (presence detection)
- Lync client for the PC to function as a simple to use communication tool for all client communication such as presence status, instant messaging, telephony, desktop sharing, and video conferencing
- The usual "look and feel" operation for employees
- Ability to use a variety of certified communication devices such as audio devices for the PC workstations, video conferencing systems, and also mobile devices for mobile working
- Lync client and web conferencing client from a single user interface
- Full unified communications capabilities on nearly every mobile platform; including Microsoft Windows Phone, Microsoft Surface, Google Android, Apple IPad, IPhone, and so on
- Communication integration with Microsoft Outlook and other Microsoft Office applications

- Full use of the solution in a secure and compliant manner from the Internet

- Use of the solution among all independent companies (for example, vendor companies, sister and cooperating companies, business partners, and so on) that use the Office Communications Server, Lync Server, or Microsoft Lync online in Microsoft's Office 365 cloud offering

- SIP Carrier Connection options that enable multimedia communication with companies that have UC solutions from other manufacturers

- Development platform that allows the integration of UC capabilities with other enterprise applications through documented APIs and interfaces such as **Unified Communications Web App (UCWA)** or **Unified Communications Managed API (UCMA)**

For more information on UCWA and UCMA, go to `http://channel9.msdn.com/posts/Lync-Developer-Roundtable-UCWA-Overview` and `http://ucwa.lync.com/`.

- It is a software-based solution that makes no special demands for server hardware so that previously purchased server hardware can still be used at Contoso; this also includes the ability to deploy the UC solution in a virtualized server environment or in the future as a "hybrid" solution if certain areas of Lync is used as a cloud service

- Migration plan in stages allows the introduction of Microsoft UC to be gradually integrated into Contoso

Upon evaluation, the UC solution from Microsoft has probably the highest degree of alignment to the needs of Contoso; considering the operating needs of the employee, the functionality of the solution, and the impact of the introduction of such a solution to the company are then examined. To be fair, other well-known manufacturers also offer innovative solutions and products in this space. The ability to execute an integration of high-end video conferencing, instant messaging, presence integration, virtual/online meeting, and the integration with social networking elements or platforms is part of other solutions as well. Other good examples would be solutions offered by Cisco, IBM, Avaya, or those in the hosted space (hosting solutions) such as Google, VSee, and Netviewer.

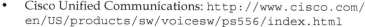

Refer the following URLs for more information:

- Cisco Unified Communications: `http://www.cisco.com/en/US/products/sw/voicesw/ps556/index.html`
- IBM Unified Communications: `http://www-935.ibm.com/services/us/en/it-services/converged-communications-services.html`
- Avaya Unified Communications: `http://www.avaya.com/usa/portfolios/unified-communications/`
- Google Talk: `http://www.google.com/talk/`
- VSee "Unified Communications/Remote Working": `http://vsee.com/`
- Netviewer: `http://www.netviewer.com/en/`

Without underestimating any of the available solutions from other manufacturers (and I really think every available platform has advantages and of course limitations), Microsoft offers the "deepest" integration into Microsoft products. In other words, the integration of UC into Outlook, SharePoint, CRM, or even custom developed applications is an absolute differentiator for Microsoft Lync. Additionally, the backend system for Lync is relatively compact. Depending on the complexity of the UC integration, the environment can be also very complex but Microsoft Lync offers a large portion of the communication and collaboration features using only a Lync Front End Server and a Lync Edge Server but we will discuss all the deployment options for small, medium, or enterprise business in *Chapter 8, Technology Inside the Microsoft UC Platform and a Look into the Future*. To summarize, at this point, Lync is "easier" to integrate, more manageable, and requires relatively less hardware (number of potential servers in a standard deployment) for the integration and deployment process, compared to other UC platforms and solutions available in the market.

Additional benefits of UC solution

Back to the benefits that Contoso would gain out of the "right" UC solution. The business case for Contoso is a mix of integrating "shorter/faster" ways for communication, collaboration, eliminating fixed locations for employees and staff, and converting different communication channels into a less expensive software-based communication solution for use both inside and outside the company.

The main priorities in the business case for Contoso's new UC platform are shown as follows:

- **Reduce travel costs** by web conferencing, presentations, and online meetings.

- **Resolution of S2M connections** to the public ISDN, since access by carriers are over SIP trunks. In other words, using SIP/VoIP connections from carriers (telecommunication services provider) instead of ISDN switches and technology.

- **Merging** the formerly separated telephony and IT departments (change project).

- **Promotion** of home offices, because the solution allows the unrestricted use of the Internet, which in turns also allows the employees to ensure a better harmony between work and family.

- **The introduction of mobile working** can allow Contoso to offer improved employment opportunities for parents after the birth of a child. This also opens up the option to employ experts from remote locations, although their activities would usually end up with a move to the vicinity of the main office. However, they are able to have their employees live in lower-cost residential areas which are further away from the city center as they need only to visit to the office on certain days of the week.

- **Reduce business-related CO2 emissions** as employees do not have to travel to work every day since home working is possible. This also reduces the cost of fuel for the company car for trips to the workplace and for meetings with customers and business partners.

This "green factor" is another advantage that enterprise companies should not underestimate. Some of the world's most famous and successful companies face a lot of pressure to demonstrate a green business strategy. Information Technology and Telecommunications can dramatically help to achieve this and support the company in meeting their green strategy, resulting in a better competitive reputation.

- **Reduce office space** since 100 percent of the employees need not be in the office all the time (Shared Desk Principle).

Reduction in office space is an important factor that has even been implemented by Microsoft. The Microsoft subsidiary in Switzerland and Austria, Europe planned their new offices for only a certain percentage of all employees. In other words, if employees need to meet customers and business partners, they can come to the office and use the office space. Since office space is limited, up to 30 percent of all employees use their home office instead. The advantages are that it saves space, energy cost, and cost for other equipment. In exchange, we achieve more flexibility, modern "work" culture, and higher efficiency.

- **Reduction of roaming charges** for mobile phones as employees who are on business trips abroad can now make long conference calls using the Lync client and a PC with an Internet access.

- **Reduction of fees for external conference call** providers as Lync Server can be used as a dial-in conference server as well.

- **Optimization** of the communication and collaboration interface and workflow with customers, business partners, and employees. UC optimizes waiting time, availability, and even communication among all parties. In other words, it increases the productivity factor of employees and customers (Contoso communication and collaboration interface).

- Ability to have additional product specialists for the field staff to **provide customer support** for special products through desktop sharing and video conferencing with customers.

From decision, Proof of Concept, to rollout of UC

After the RFP process, the decision to "go" with one selected UC solution is usually the start of the "Proof of Concept" stage. However, based on the facts presented and the knowledge of other reference (deployment) projects from other companies, the **Chief Executive Officer (CEO)** can decide to start with the full introduction of the UC solution from Microsoft and to run the POC inside the production environment of the company immediately. In many organizations, the decision brings the POC into a production rollout to every end user comes only after a successful POC.

In some other projects such as Contoso, the organizational environment and the business division were already prepared before the technical part of the project started. Both ways are absolutely valid to start a communications and collaborations project and especially in more complex environments such as enterprise companies, it is sometimes more important to start with the "organizational" preparation process so that it gets aligned with the change management process within the company.

To prepare this step from a business perspective, the human resource department in Contoso also put a reward system in place. The idea was to reward managers inside the organization who enforce and support the implementation of the new communication interface. It also rewarded employees who changed their communication and collaboration behavior using the new software-based platform. This step was important to get all the necessary support for this project by the required parties, to shorten the time required to achieve the return on investment and to push the necessary change management process from within the company.

For this company, the introduction of the solution is accompanied by:

- Development of a usage-based loyalty program that rewards the use of web conferencing
- Development of a bonus program for managers who can manage a large number of successful employees with home offices
- A combination option to work from both home and office
- Possibility to work across different platforms, including mobile devices
- Development of a multimedia utility model, which will replace the traditional phone billing
- Development of a call volume model that compares the fees paid today for those calls to the new costs using the SIP carrier — to identify the most cost efficient SIP carrier
- Employee training through classroom and online training courses to show the added value in the operation
- Development of a user agreement by the Human Resource department to regulate the use of presence information
- Selection of the pilot area, as the reference group for the intended introduction of the UC solution
- Development of a user model to estimate the additive load that is coming to the existing data network

- Development of a plan for the integration of non-PC workstations such as fax machines, telephones at the reception, and so on

- Creation of an organizational diagram according to the IT organizational structure after the implementation of the UC project

The pilot phase

First of all, Contoso decided to order the required server hardware that was recommended in the system integrator's design proposal together with the Microsoft Lync architect. The server hardware was a mix of "physical" hardware and virtualized servers. The virtualized servers would host basic infrastructure and Lync services in a virtual environment.

Next, both the IT department as well as the user can start preparations for the real integration. A 50-member department in the main office was changed to act as the pilot group for the first stage in the UC pilot. These 50 users were made to have their existing PBX phone switched off. The telephone numbers of these pilot users were routed through a S2M (ISDN) connection between the Siemens HiPath Routed 4000 PBX system and the SIP gateway which is connected to the Lync Server (Mediation Server).

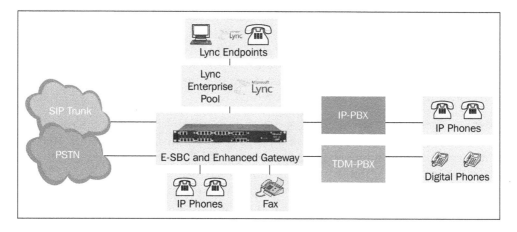

The preceding graphic is an example for VoIP Gateway (AudioCodes); connection between Lync, PBX, PSTN (telephony network), and/or SIP (IP) Trunking at: http://www.audiocodes.com/solutions/microsoft/sbcs-and-gateways.

For more information on the Siemens HiPath 4000 system go to:
`http://www.siemens-enterprise.com/us/products-`
`services/voice-solutions/hipath4000.aspx`.

In additional to the "Enterprise Voice" integration between Lync and the existing PBX solution, the goal was to also implement the Internet-facing Lync Edge Server to provide mobile employees the possibility to work from everywhere, including working from home. Another part of the POC was to establish a connection between the selected customers and business partners to test if a "Federation" between Lync and Office Communications Server environment is valuable for the daily business. The selected federated companies were also part of the **User Acceptance Testing (UAT)** phase of the project as well as the Lync platform tests and verification by the IT department.

Each user of the pilot group was given a certified Lync USB handset, headset, or Bluetooth device and of course, the Lync application (client) on all available platforms for tablet and/or PC users. Contoso had to also make a list of the Top 5 positive and negative experiences for a week. It is important that when choosing a pilot group, the group selected must work closely together so they can experience the benefits of working well together. Randomly choosing a pilot group of managers, for example, who do not cooperate with each other every day, contributes little to the general acceptance of the solution. Another tip is to choose an innovative and more agile type of employees for the pilot. It is important to also have critical feedback during a Lync or UC project and always remember to win the trust and support of the divisions. For example, you do not force a telecommunication division to use a new tool and create panic/fear since this group of employees is used to the legacy equipment. You must win them over slowly.

It is also important to implement a good communication process for the pilot as well as for the upcoming rollout to all other employees inside the organization. The dedicated project management team was responsible in the coordination process between the system integrator (implementation partner) and the consulting services contact at Microsoft. The implementation itself was realized by the system integrator but for quality assurance, Contoso has decided to hire a technical Lync Architect from Microsoft.

In an ideal scenario, everyone should be onboard and with the project, it is important to share their positive experience across other teams, share positive and constructive feedback with others, build up supporters inside the organization to promote support for the project, and evangelize the efficiency and the value for everyone inside the company. Some other organizations have more innovative ideas, they reward their employees additionally with "travel saving points", UC/innovation awards for groups, teams, individuals, or also "goodies" in the form of new communication devices, tablet PCs with integrated audio and video equipment to get them ready for "UC" meetings.

The pilot phase demonstrated the following results:

- Over the six week trial period, the Top 5 lists changed significantly.

- Actual adoption by the employees was better than the estimation derived from the response of the management and the UC project team during the initial planning phase. Perhaps this is because their employees fall into the age groups that desire more flexibility in their "daily" work with customers and business partners.

- The most frequently mentioned negative comments did not state that working with the new technology appears to be impossible.

- User training and follow up with the "trained" user groups were required. The user groups were asked to participate in question-and-answer sessions to ensure that the UC platform is used efficiently. Documentation and video/webcast training content were also shared on a SharePoint site to provide users a comprehensive curriculum.

- Even the most discerning user would still not go back to their phone and also preferred using the new certified Lync devices (selected devices in this case were the Jabra, Plantronics, and Sennheiser audio devices). It is possible that the adoption of devices has improved the adoption of this new Lync application. Another possibility is that many people around that user were excited, excessive criticism of the new changes makes the user appear backward to those around them. To avoid such a stigma, they would rather not go back to the old way.

- Involved customers and business partners also supported the positive change to have a better communication and collaboration interface with contacts inside the Contoso organization. Through Federation or instant messaging connectivity, other organizations have the advantage to "ping" and "instant message" their sales, technical sales, or audiences in the Contoso management—at no cost on the telecommunication side!

Implementation of training

As mentioned previously, an important factor for success of the UC pilot was adequate training for pilot users, end users, train the trainer program, management/executives, and other special users. Not only in the pilot phase of a project but also as a permanent available resource in the UC training portal where it is available anytime. Other great options are one page description for all types of users, training for administrators, and IT-specialists, recorded mini videos that demonstrate all major features of the UC solution, and extended documentation on the internal SharePoint website. Successful UC projects always have shown a successful training plan and onboarding list of employees for the new UC solution. Another good idea is to implement a recurring "UC" newsletter in the company on how the organization benefits for the new technology and what the progress, rollout, and roadmap looks like for unified communications at Contoso. All of these factors helped dramatically to achieve a faster positive ROI for the project.

The overall concept

The overall concept was simple. With the support of the CEO, an eternal migration phase was avoided. Hence, high costs were avoided. All PC workstations, tablet PCs, and mobile devices were installed with the Microsoft Lync client software. Users could choose from a range of Lync certified USB hand, headsets, and Bluetooth devices by Jabra, Plantronics, and Sennheiser. Non-PC workstations (lobby telephones, telephones at the reception, fax machines, and so on) are now connected by the SIP Carrier IP Centrex extensions and have the same or a similar set of features needed for their "daily" business. Contoso implemented, at this point, special training for all employees who use the lobby phones and fax devices.

 Microsoft provides a wide set of certified devices, a list of which is available here: http://technet.microsoft.com/en-us/lync/gg278164.aspx.

Based on the UC platform, context-sensitive communication in the insurance professional program (an LOB application), instant messaging, and presence information function were integrated into the customer extranet web portal, allowing more effective communication among employees themselves as well as with the customers. The integration of web chat via Lync 2013 UCWA and simple "web" presence is shown as follows:

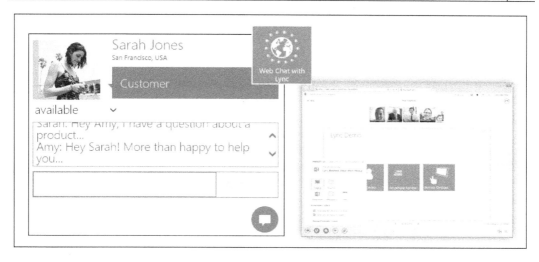

Contoso used the Microsoft SharePoint technology to create an "extranet web portal" and has plans to migrate this to a Microsoft-hosted Office 365 online solution to achieve further business and technical benefits.

Another important task was the creation of software policies for archiving and enhanced reporting of all communication modalities. Similar to the "old" Siemens telephony system which offers a reporting and business intelligence interface, Lync and unified communications enables an efficient software-based way to access call detail reports, VoIP network benchmarks, and the archiving of important communication. Contoso would implement this step in the next project which will be realized after the full rollout of Microsoft Lync 2013. The monitoring and reporting of Lync can also help the project determine the details of the usage of Lync voice, video, chat, sharing, and so on during the pilot phase. It would also be possible to use this information and compare it with existing reports from the legacy environment to see how much of the "usage" has changed from legacy equipment to the new environment. The reports can also be used to identify potential quality issues, for example on the network and VoIP side. In other reference projects, project teams compared reporting data of different communication modalities to find out what the preferred way of communication is for their users; for example whether chat was preferred over voice communication or even the phone. This kind of change of communication can demonstrate an interesting aspect of the return of investment for such projects and also show how users change their communication and collaboration preferences based on the available technology—this changes the innovation factor of the organization or company itself.

Another optional extension is to implement Lync into the customer care space of Contoso. For this Contoso is evaluating Lync certified solution providers who are offering an extension of all types of communication and collaboration modalities to support an integration of Contoso's contact center and customer facing support. With this level of integration, Contoso will be able to offer additional external UC-based communication to customers and to support with instant messaging, web chat, screen sharing, or also call back solutions to increase the customers' satisfaction and to achieve an even better ROI. They have also managed to shift the traditional legacy contact center solution that was based on Siemens technology to a UC-enabled or integrated contact center platform. Due to the complexity of this project, it was a good decision by the Contoso leadership team to start a dedicated project (and RFP process) after the official close of the initial Lync integration project. At this point, they have also completely merged the Siemens PBX system into a native Lync environment via SIP trunking from a certified telecommunication service provider.

Concluding remarks

The company Contoso is now prepared for the next stage of multimedia communication with employees, customers, and partners, possible extension to their customer care space and more importantly integration options with other LOB applications such as a full CRM desktop and other usage scenarios.

The scalability of the UC solution and the full, nomadic way of communication provides the company tremendous flexibility and a high ROI. Increased flexibility and satisfaction among employees also greatly helps in the hiring of new staff and to be innovative enough to attract the next generation of information workers for Contoso. This reference story demonstrated the innovation power of Contoso as compared to other competitors in the market and the early adoption of modern communication, collaboration. In the future, we might see the integration of social networking components inside the company.

Another important factor was to implement a company-wide standard for IT and Telecommunications equipment and also for mobile platforms like the Microsoft's Windows Phone technology. With this step, Contoso further implemented an efficient way to bring e-mail integration, real-time communication, and also collaboration in the form of mobile SharePoint integration to all Windows mobile phones. For this, Contoso offered several different types of Windows Phones on the internal SharePoint website and every employee had the choice to pick their own phone from the available devices. The hardware was preconfigured and has the mobile UC integration like the Lync mobile client, SharePoint, (Microsoft) SkyDrive Pro integration, and so on included. Employees across different business divisions welcomed the change and this new benefit of using a new hardware with satisfaction instead of being frustrated by technical limitations.

The overall required time for the project, including RFP process was less than 10 months. The business partner and system integrator, in other words the consultant, was then paid a project fee based on a percentage of the actual savings and achievements for this project. The consultant from Microsoft was paid for part of the workload in the support agreement between Contoso and Microsoft and had only limited expenses including travel expenses to Contoso. The same business partner/system integrator, as mentioned, was engaged to do a network performance and environment availability assessment six months after the initial implementation. The goal was to run stress tests of the Lync and network environment and to see if any other investment needs to be planned on the infrastructure and networking side.

For Contoso, the unified communications project was an absolute success and based on this milestone, they have many other opportunities to extend their new UC platform into other types of business communication to customers and business partners. If you are interested in other successful UC projects or even reference projects, you should visit the Microsoft Lync homepage (`http://lync.microsoft.com`). Companies such as Lionbridge, Boeing, Dell, Nikon, and many others have already taken advantage of the successful implementation of Microsoft Lync and provided some high level information of the integration and the choice of implementation partner (system integrator) on their website.

The following screenshot from `http://lync.microsoft.com` illustrates Microsoft Lync portal with important information and content:

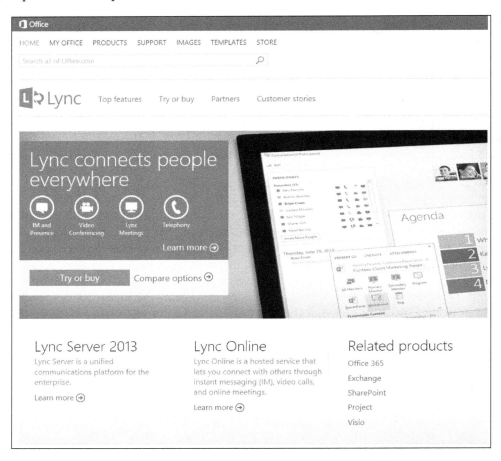

Summary

This chapter described a real project which shows the evaluation and realization of a unified communication project. In other projects where the CEO is not directly involved to drive a change in the IT and Telecommunications infrastructure to UC, a strong business case is needed by the middle layer of management to present potential cost savings, increase customer satisfaction, and display innovation as compared to other competitors. In other words, highlight the competitive advantage and also demonstrate a compelling ROI and TCO.

Chapters in this book have provided information to help build such required documentation and planning but it is necessary to have the overall stakeholder support for such important changes in the collaboration and communication infrastructure.

There are many important lessons learnt from UC project implementations. What did Contoso and other companies who have implemented UC projects learn from this experience? What kind of information and knowledge would you need to plan, design, and execute a UC project?

In the next chapter, we will dive into this topic and summarize the most important points for you. We will approach this from different perspectives — technology as well as organizational and business. Find out more in the next chapter.

7
Analyzing the Key Points of a Unified Communications Project

The previous chapter provided us a great customer example of how unified communications, Lync, was successfully deployed and implemented as a platform for communication and collaboration for the company, Contoso. As mentioned in the previous chapter, it is absolutely important to have a detailed analysis and assessment of the company's business and technical requirements as part of the overall evaluation process for a sustainable successful UC project. It is also important to have responsible business and professional people to conduct proper planning before reaching the RFP process or actual project. The truth is many technical projects fail in mid or enterprise organizations. In fact, failure can occur during any stages of the project. Be it the evaluation phase of a specific technology, during the RFP process, at the project execution phase itself, or even before any of these stages, failure can happen because the business case was not done professionally. We not only see such high failure rates for projects in the telecommunication space but also in projects involving new areas such as cloud technology. There are many reasons and factors that determine whether a project becomes successful or not. We will discuss the most important areas in this chapter:

- Evaluation phase for UC projects
- Business case and business justification
- Bringing the management onboard for a UC project
- RFP process and selecting a solution provider

- Pilot or proof of concept phase – what does success look like?
- Adoption of UC inside the organization
- Cost, licensing, SLA, and official end of a project

At the end of this chapter, a summary of the current best practices and learning will also be provided.

Evaluation phase

It is often in the evaluation phase that mistakes happen and these mistakes usually surface later as challenging problems for the UC project. In the previous chapter we have seen the term **Request for Proposal (RFP)** under the evaluation phase. However, before we can put together an RFP document, we must first find out what the company's business and technical requirements and the communication and collaboration strategy looks like.

How can this be done easily?

Most companies conduct a survey of their staff and management to find out the satisfaction level of their current IT and communication platform as well as what they would like to have in the new solution based on their needs and preferences. Some other companies already have a "new" communication and collaboration strategy in place and are already aware of requirements for an adequate UC solution and project. As we see more and more UC, cloud, social networking, and mobile platform projects popping up in every region, it seems like an evolutional topic that companies have in their implementation plan by investing in business consultants and comparing their communication interfaces with those of other competitors and market players.

As a consultant with clients in various industries and geographical areas around the globe, the most common starting point I have seen is that the companies let their IT departments run their own initiatives without inviting other company divisions and departments. They engage professional consulting services from an independent consulting company or solution provider, which is a good thing. However, the IT departments often request a complex integration of the entire company's information technology system as the starting point. Then they realize that they did not have the support of the other departments and their management and they did not have the necessary budget to purchase the solution and to pay for other applicable third-party services.

Another issue here is that IT department usually forgets to analyze all business requirements or to understand their business benefits. When business divisions are made to work with the IT department on a business case for the project, we often noticed that the business divisions have difficulties understanding their own business requirements and most of the time they are clueless about the functionalities and capabilities of the communication and collaboration platform. One key learning point of many organizations is that most IT departments are not fully capable to drive an innovation project alone. Instead, it is highly recommended to have a consultant with both technical and business background to lead the UC project. Support from their management, budgetary limits, lack communication to business divisions, or are too much focused comparing unified communication with the existing legacy system that is in place could affect the success of the project.

This is not the situation we would like for our end users, partners, and of course, the manufacturers of the solution. Before we start analyzing the different areas of most common "mistakes" or "deficiencies and issues" with UC projects, let us first summarize the most common key problem areas:

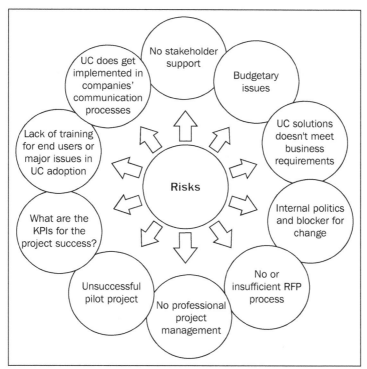

Key issues and blockers for technology projects inside a company

To counteract or entirely prevent such a situation, it is necessary to consult with other business divisions, departments, and their own management. The first conversations must be about an upcoming project in a constructive way, where responsibilities are clarified and the project has the support of management and the people who are responsible. It is also very important to identify the business cases well with all soft data and hard facts such as financial data, ROI, and TCO estimations. This is usually very important because most UC projects are not successful or do not get "approved" and are bought into it by the management only as an innovative idea to have something new or to have more functionalities. For enterprise companies, it is also important to involve other stakeholders from important key areas such as Telecommunications, customer care, sales, business development, human resources, and IT security/compliance. It is extremely important to receive a "sign off" by all required stakeholders otherwise any UC project would be at risk from the very beginning. Past projects have shown that a bottom-up strategy does not work in most cases. In other words, the IT department cannot drive an innovation project and present it to the upper management later on to receive attention, resources, and full support from a business side. Another important aspect to take care of is to always have support from the stakeholders and management during UC projects and not to lose the traction and ongoing involvement from the pilot phase all the way through project execution. What you definitely do not want is to receive the initial sign off, you start the project but later on it gets blocked for example by the telecommunications division or slowed down by an uncooperative IT department.

An ideal situation is as follows: The management wants an optimization of the information and communication technology and this "order" is communicated by the management to the respective departments from the beginning. Also, the management or a responsible topic/project owner has already identified potential savings or has a high-level business justification for the migration to UC enabled communication scenarios. In this case, it changes the need for a common agreement and vote because the project has complete support from the management. In most cases, this support comes together with the budget and thus would definitely allow you to worry less.

At this point, being able to put together a compelling business case about savings, increased communication with customers and business partners to the management is most important. Even if the management makes a "technology" based decision to have a new collaboration and communication interface available for the company, it is necessary to have a business case prepared for any future discussion. In other words, it is important to research on other reference projects on the internet to see how other companies and perhaps how your competitors have implemented an innovative unified communications project successfully and what key results they have achieved. Most UC projects I have seen struggled coming up with a "real" business case. Some of the challenges include collecting accurate and reliable financial data from numerous business divisions. If you think about UC in terms of faster workflows, a communication and collaboration process or a potential increase in satisfaction for customers, business partners as well as the internal employees), it is very often difficult to draft a 100 percent detailed business case for all potential areas of improvement. Speaking from my own UC project experiences, I have learned that the management is always impressed by a mix of innovation factors and cost savings or an improvement in a specific benchmark KPI, such as customer satisfaction, and competitive advantage, for their business.

Let us use a hypothetical example to show how we can create a business case at this point. Back to the example of Contoso, we saw an implementation of different communication and collaboration modalities. Based on the assumption that the business consultant or internal project related resources have done their job well, we would know how the collaboration scenario would look like before the project ends and we would have a rough picture on the potential improvements.

In this example, we shall calculate the improvement in customers handling time for Contoso's marketing division only. Contoso advertising specialists make an average of 60,000 calls per month and require an estimate of 15 minutes for every call to identify the customer, get all required information (customer ID, budget status, explain products and solutions to customer, and so on). Contoso's cost for the current workflow without a unified communications solution is 450,000 USD per month and 5,400,000 USD per fiscal year.

An adequate business case would be to provide a better collaboration and communication "tool" for Contoso's marketing/advertising specialists and to provide a more qualitative reporting back to the Contoso's management. In this scenario, the business consultant evaluated the current scenario without UC for Contoso and compared the potential improvement using Lync 2013 with the ability to have the following:

- VoIP calls from a single application

- Enhanced communication modalities: Desktop sharing from customers to Contoso advertising specialists (Through Lync web client/**Unified Communications Web App (UCWA)**)

- Integration of Line of Business application **Customer Relationship Management (CRM)** software together with Lync 2013 to provide all customers' information to Contoso

The following screenshot shows the business case example in detail:

	Benefits	Description	Current Cost/minute	Call Volume per month	Minutes per Call Savings	Overall minutes/month	$$$ Cost factor/month	$$$ Cost factor/year	Cost Saving/year	ROI (%)
Todays Scenario at Contoso	Currently an average of 15 minutes per customer case/call	Employees receive a phone call or make a phone call to customers for advertising reasons	0.5	60,000	15	900,000	450,000	5,400,000		
Business Case with Lync (voice only)	Cost Reduction to an average of 8 minutes per customer case/call (reduction of 7 minutes per customer case/call)	Employees are using Lync for phone calls / Employees reduce the amount of required time per call based on faster call handling, desktop sharing, LOB integration	0.5	60,000	8	480,000	250,000	2,880,000	2,520,000	47

It is a 12-month period over which a company budgets its spending. A fiscal year may run over any period of 12 months and does not necessarily correspond to a calendar year. It is also a period that a company or government uses for calculating annual ("yearly") financial statements for accounting purposes and preparing financial statements in businesses and other organizations.

In the preceding example, we can see that Contoso has an average cost of 0.50 USD per call and has the potential to save an estimate of 7 minutes per call with a customer. This business case could realize a potential savings of 2,520,000 USD and a ROI of 47 percent in the first fiscal year. Of course this example is just a very high-level overview of a real detailed business case but based on my experience, this would be a good starting point for business consultants, program managers, or project managers. The same kind of calculation could be done for IM, video conferencing, reduction of travel cost, and so on. These are some of the potential cost savings and benefits, which we have covered in *Chapter 5, Cost Optimization Approaches*, already.

Of course, such calculations have to be included in a management style presentation deck for presenting and convincing stakeholders and management on the need for a UC project.

In some cases, research also uncovers additional opportunities to innovate in addition to the initial project for other key business areas of the own organization. This could be then be included in the next stage planning for other "types" of integration with Lync or with another UC technology.

Next to this, it is also recommended to prepare a scorecard for the upcoming UC project. This scorecard should demonstrate all major goals that have to be achieved in the project and could be used as documentation for ongoing communication and status presentation back to the management.

Additionally, it is also important to know how the environment looks like. Many projects fail because desktop computers or the mix of mobile devices does not support an efficient integration of the UC technology. Also high availability needs to be discussed with the management. It is important to know how the **Service Level Agreement (SLA)** looks like and if additional changes of the network or IT infrastructure environment need to be part of the preparation of a UC implementation.

The next step is getting together to form a project team within the company. The project team should have a responsible project leader with appropriate project experience and several selected qualified employees. In some projects, the best way to go about this is to hire an external contractor, who will be responsible for the project management and the execution, to work with all available resources and to track the project in all required ways. Real project examples have shown that an external person is sometimes also a success factor since this new team member is a neutral party and does not belong to any particular division. Every organization has its own drive, positive spirit, and has many different teams. But to increase the chances of the project being successful, an external project manager can prevent these different teams from bringing their internal differences into this project.

An estimate of the cost is also relevant at this point because in the course of evaluating a realistic project budget solution, budget planning is also part of the process (For example, whether funds would be provided by the IT department or would it be taken out from budget reserves should be made transparent)

Some companies at this point have already received the previous pledged funds from other departments that have been allocated to the various cost centers of the future UC project. For example, IT, trade, and telecommunications department can all help to share the cost. Another possible source of funding could be obtained by finding out if there are any current budgets planned to update or maintain legacy equipment. If there are, such projects could be put on hold and merged into the overall UC project to replace "old" and legacy technology instead of maintaining an outdated equipment.

The next step is to analyze your needs. Determination of the requirements is best done through surveys, interviews, studies, and as mentioned before the project – reference stories. For example, surveys by e-mail, internal information events, interviews with communities and working groups conducted by independent external consulting companies, and collecting evidence from other projects. An additional way would be to work with an external business consultant on an internal assessment on how the communication and collaboration processed needs to be optimized and what kind of technology could meet those additional requirements. There are also many companies who are specialists in UC, collaboration, and cloud technology. These companies offer **Communication Enabled Business Process (CEBP)** workshops to their customers to help them analyze all the communication and collaboration processes in their company. This would help them create an impactful business case and justification. It is also a great opportunity for them to clarify all technical requirements and to identify challenging areas that they would expect during execution. Some large enterprise companies also worked with external research companies to demonstrate how the evolutional change in collaboration and communication with their customers is required and presented the results back to their management to get the approval or support for a targeted real-time collaboration and communication project. Such research materials also usually come with a list of manufacturers who have the ability to deliver a complete unified communications platform and this knowledge can be also used for the RFP process.

These findings should be filtered again and the resulting requirements are prioritized to into primary and secondary requirements. At this point, a Request for Proposal (RFP) document is generated to show the requirements and to construct a potential case study for the various departments.

Purpose for the RFP document are as follows:

- A document to inform suppliers that an organization is looking to procure and encourages them to make their best effort.

- Specifications on what the suppliers need to submit for the RFP process, such as equipment that needs to be purchase. If requirements are available, it can also be incorporated into the document.

- Alerts suppliers that the selection process for a specific solution or system integrator is competitive.

- The RFP is usually written for a broad set of companies in the market for distribution and response.

Reasons for a RFP process are as follows:

- To ensure that suppliers can respond factually to the identified requirements

- To have a structured evaluation and selection procedure so that an organization can demonstrate impartiality — a crucial factor in public sector procurements

The RFP document should cover the following areas:

- Overview and business justification; the overall goal of the proposed project should be summarized.

- Information about the company and organization; this level of information is not part of every RFP document but it helps the business partner or potential system integrator/manufacturer to understand the organization (such as location, size, and financial status)

- A detailed overview about the current environment in terms of telecommunication equipment, network environment, and the overall IT infrastructure.

- A detailed description of the planned scenario; this is important to explain the ideal future scenario that should be the outcome of the proposed project.

- A detailed list of all technical requirements, scenarios, features, functions, interfaces to current technical environment, location of IT, and telecommunication equipment, and so on. This here is the main part of the RFP document and should list everything that the company (or the IT/telecommunications team) requires in terms of a solution or the integration of the UC platform/solution itself.

- Explanation about risks, timeline, budget scope, and other requirements. This content should be also part of the RFP because it is important that a business partner can orientate based on the timeline and risk level of the project. Some business partner might have concerns because of the SLA requirements or the timeline for execution on the project. This needs to be clarified in this section of the RFP document.

Next to the listed areas of required content, there is some other important information that should be part of the RFP document (also sometimes a section that explains what happens if a project is not successful.) RFP documents are quite "flexible", in other words there are many different versions and thoughts for a structure and content for RFP documents in the market but I think the overall and common need is always to describe the current and the future state with all requirements. There are very good samples for RFP documents on the web and can be used as template for the RFP process. As mentioned before, a RFP documentation and process should always be driven by the "right" person. This probably sounds strange. In a big organization, it should always be the procurement team who understands the requirements well and formulates them into a RFP document. In small companies it should perhaps be a technical business consultant and not their own IT or telecommunication division. This consultant can be internal but ideally is an external consultant for the project. The reason for that is clear; the RFP process should be neutral as possible and not be driven by specific interests of one business division or should also not point out to a specific solution in the market. It is also important that all requirements are formulated in the right way and usually a dedicated responsible owner in procurement or a consultant delivers a more adequate version of this important RFP documentation.

All requirements and scenarios in the document should then again be presented by the project managers to the management in a so-called project-management or board meeting. The aim is to obtain awareness from the management and also for them to provide constructive feedback. Depending on the legal situation and corporate structure, this version of the RFP or tender document can already be used as an official advertisement or a request to solution providers for further processing. During RFP process, it is important to target all potential business partners or "UC" manufacturers in a neutral way. The RFP process is an important step-by-step decision making process of the key offerings and technologies.

A real learning out of RFP processes and documents is that it is very important to involve the right parties and perhaps external support resources on this. Examples have shown that enterprise companies sometimes have generated RFP documents out of templates for other legacy technology projects and they went into a completely wrong direction in trying to accomplish a comparison of unified communications related features and scenarios mapped to what is known as the "old" PBX platforms and solutions. This is one of the main factors why sometimes legacy equipment only gets updated to a newer version, instead of migrating to an innovative technology for the next generation of companywide communication and collaboration. Additionally, it is also required to have close conversations and team work with the procurement team or division in the company on how the selection process should progress and to have the ability for clarification if certain business requirements are not clear enough. One last item which is important at this stage is that the RFP process and documentation needs to be driven by the right team inside or outside the company! Real examples have showed that it is the IT and sometimes the Telecommunications division who are afraid of change end up trying to get another (newer) version of a legacy technology in place. Some of the projects end up presenting incorrect information back to the management, so with the wrong information, the management end up making a wrong decision and invest in an expensive traditional telephony project.

Selecting unified communications solution and solution provider

When the RFP process is established and finalized, we move on to the next step. After establishing contact with selected solution providers, the default procedure is to have presentation and demonstration by the respective solution or technology providers. So make sure that there are not too many suppliers selected at the beginning because the long selection and evaluation phase may result in additional fees. This is a very important success factor. It is important to involve the most important UC technologies in the RFP but do not go over the limit! It is inefficient to compare 50 different solutions. It is recommended that under certain circumstances, the vendors are given the RFP document in advance to prepare themselves before they come back to you for a meeting discussion or you can prepare a summarized list from the RFP for the vendors so that you are able to quickly identify their capabilities. Also at this stage, let us take care that the selection process is not driven by the status of relationship with a certain business partner. In other words, the procurement team or the business consultant should ensure that a specific solution or a specific business partner does not get preferential status, unless their solution or platform matches all the business requirements of the upcoming project.

In the first presentation, the supplier is cross-examined for the validity of unified communications solutions. Therefore, always have a technology competent person from the project team included in these presentations and remember to ask if they have reference customers, examples on specific business cases or other important content for further decision in the "right" technology. After the first round of presentations, the project team should make a selection of three or more suppliers and have a more in-depth discussion with them. In the second round, the following topics should be discussed: explicit details of departments, extension capabilities, integration effort, product or solution roadmap, integration opportunities of other areas (social networking, contact center/customer care, application development and extensibility), support by supplier or recommended partners, customer reference visits, cost estimate of licensing, calculation of the **Return On Investment (ROI)** or **Total Cost of Ownership (TCO)**, travel cost savings, communication cost savings, and the possibility of future development of the solution with support assurance.

It is also recommended to document all meetings and conversations with potential suppliers, especially to create and document a matrix of the features and scenario based functional comparison. We want to match the features and scenarios to the financial benefits. Some companies map out their required communication and collaboration features to the business case to understand potential savings and other aspects of the ROI. If you want to implement UC into other areas of the company, for example a contact center, sales, and marketing division, it is useful to include the language of finance, ROI, and TCO in addition to the technological benefits of a UC project.

To summarize this important part of the process: All requirements, business case and business justification needs to be very clear after the management gives the "approval" for the proposed project inside the organization. It does not matter whether it is the IT or telecommunication business division inside the company that is responsible for the requirements. For all sizes of projects, especially medium to enterprise projects, all requirements must get formulated into an RFP document and driven by the right business consultant in the procurement team. The selection process should include all involved solution providers, system integrators, or platform and solution manufacturers. Selection should be purely based on the trust of the solution and also on the external company itself to realize the project based on business requirements for your own company and organization.

Decision making and pilot phase

Once the decision for a solution provider has been made, the next steps for a test pilot installation in the real IT environment of the company is planned. At this point, also clarify who would realize this test environment. Some solution providers are happy to offer their specially trained presales engineers or architects and consultants who can implement these test pilots for free or at a minimal cost. The reason for this would be to test out the solution in a dedicated "test" environment, to prove if all required features and scenarios are part of the UC solution, and to check if the companies requirements are properly addressed. Another proof of concept is to realize the project in the "real" production environment of the company. This is usually a better way because the UC solution has to be part of the real IT and telecommunications environment and if any problems occur, it would be already at the pilot level something that can be fixed between the business partner and the internal project and technical team inside the company. After the test pilot phase, based on what you would like to be implemented as the final solution, it would be possible as part of the offer from the solution provider that a quotation would be given for the official project after the pilot installation. At this point the solution provider or system integrator would provide the final version of the proposal for the integration to their own company. This final version would also decide the pricing and outcome of the pilot.

Another possibility would be to work at first with the selected solution provider or system integrator, who offers a solution proposal from the start, specifying all the requirements of services, hardware, and licensing costs for the rollout before any kind of pilot or test installation would take action.

The decision process or pilot procedure is very different for UC projects. From my own experience I have seen both versions.

- **Version 1**: The cost free or limited test installation (after or without RFP) where the official decision for the rollout and project comes after the test installation

- **Version 2**: A detailed offer from a solution provider and system integrator that is selected by the company to do a pilot or to carry out the real implementation in the production environment

However, some companies also prefer to visit reference customers and installation in the decision process to see if the proposed solution is already implemented successfully in other environments. If this is the case, usually manufacturers such as Microsoft, Cisco, IBM, Google, or others are happy to assist by finding reference customers together with the solution integrator and provider to drive the decision for the "customer", in this case, for a company such as Contoso.

Let us go to the next step. You also should have the "final" dedicated project team in place. As mentioned before, the selection of a professional, experienced project manager for telecommunication and IT projects is a very important success factor. Also be sure that a project plan is signed off by stakeholders and perhaps the upper management and that the communication of next steps is in place inside the organization. If the stakeholder matrix, communication plan, and resource plan were part of the project preparation, these same documents should also be in the final stage, signed off and ready for the project.

Based on my past experience as a UC architect and business consultant, many projects were first created with the desired functionality that is integrated in a virtual test environment by a qualified integration engineer. This is generally not advisable because a pilot installation whenever possible should be integrated into the so-called real or production environment of the company (depending on technical solvability). The reason is simple: a test environment never allows the same test as the real possibility of a technology company infrastructure with all the different elements such as network, directory services, and vulnerabilities. However, if the features and functions need to be tested first, a virtual environment is the best way to do it and have the first experience of what can be expected in the "real" implementation. Some virtual environments also have the ability to execute a rollout for the UC platform after the initial pilot. In the event that a deployment in virtual environment is planned, it is also required to have a pre-assessment of the requirements for network performance, infrastructure design, and hardware resources.

Usually, the best option for a test installation, especially one that is also being used as the proof of concept, is when the integration of the UC solution is placed in the production environment with a dedicated and selected group of pilot users as mentioned before. In many cases this is the best way to test the application with all or most of the features and communication modalities in the real environment of the company. The advantage here is that users are actually working with the UC application on their production devices such as PC's, tablets, and mobile devices. Many organizations also make the decision to limit the group of test users/pilot users to restrict the usage of the POC from the being completely busy all the time as they still want to be able to test the spectrum and the actual environment for the upcoming technology.

For this reason, the design of the pilot integration and the inclusion of test users require absolute attention. To help you to plan and implement a pilot more easily, let me share a few tips with you at this point:

- The pilot phase has to be carried out closely together with the project managers, and possibly with the management, and integration engineers.

- Select pilot users who are technically oriented and are open to change. It is important that the non-technical and also tech-savvy users are not forgotten in the pilot group as they provide a very useful and a different perspective that the "techies" might have overlooked.

- Draft an agreement that regulates the use of the information with the human resource department. This can either be done in advance or right after the pilot phase, both are possible. There is a template provided in the *Appendix* for your reference. Note that this is a frequent blocker for the project.

- Make provisions for the required equipment, such as headsets, webcams, and access to video conferencing equipment and telephone equipment (IP / digital). For the pilot it is usually simple to obtain pilot devices from manufacturers and vendors such as Jabra, Plantronics, and Sennheiser. for free or with a little budget. The devices should definitely be certified and tested within the pilot.

- Enroll pilot users in the most important functions including ongoing support from the IT department and/or project team.

- Organize status meetings with the **general contractor (GC)** of the project, the integration partner and/or the manufacturer.

 GC is the person or company who is principally responsible for the project itself or other subcontracted companies (system integrators that collaborate with the GC).

- Present and engage all involved stakeholders in the project status. It is important to set up regular meetings to provide status information and updates back to the management.

- If the pilot or test installation of the unified communications solution is completed as planned, collect feedback from pilot users through questionnaires and interviews. Analyze and interpret the results. Based on the evaluation of the feedback result, the next step should be the decision for the upcoming rollout.

- Compare results with the actual business requirements to ensure that all main scenarios are evaluated.

- Review the reports for IM, voice calls, video calls, and so on to ensure that the UC platform is extensively used by end users and possible errors or technical problems are identified. Also ensure that the reporting and business intelligence interface itself works so that usage or historical data is captured Reporting might not be part of a pilot or project, this is usually optional.

- Potentially drive stress tests, enhanced environment, and UC platform assessments to ensure that everything is properly configured, enough network and infrastructure resources are available for the UC platform, and that just everything is set up in an absolute correct way.

At this point, it is obvious that it is important that all stakeholders and the project team are satisfied with the technology, the results of user surveys, and the coverage of our own requirements. Otherwise, if the result of the pilot integration does not meet the requirements, and the integration partners and manufacturers are not able to resolve any gaps in the request at all, it would be required to focus probably on another UC solution in the worst case or to re-negotiate the price again if certain areas cannot be addressed and if the project team decides to continue with the current solution.

To be clear, a proof of concept should demonstrate the ability to address all requirements with the selected solution. In some cases, the solution does not meet the requirements and an alternative needs to be considered. Examples that the UC solution does not deliver all the features include the inability to have specific functions such as Enterprise Voice integration, that are unable to integrate with a specific line of business application or specific performance issue such as being unable to have a good connection between offices and branch office locations, and so on.

The RFP and planning process, especially a test installation or proof of concept would usually show the result of proper mapping of requirements and possible features/scenarios for the integration with the selected UC solution. However, real projects can be complex and sometimes failure can occur. In the worst case, customers need to evaluate other UC solution or "live" with the limitations but always try to re-negotiate the financial terms of the project first with the selected solution provider or system integrator. As mentioned earlier, this would be the worst-case situation. In most cases, this should not occur with a sturdy RFP process, good evaluation during the pilot/proof of concept phase, a proper set up of the project team, reliable external consulting, plus professional implementation of the pilot project with the support of all stakeholders, including the person in-charge of the budget.

Additionally, it is also a good practice to double check that all required reporting and business intelligence capabilities are in place. What you do not want is that you have all communication and collaboration features and scenarios in place but missed out on reporting some important items or it was overlooked during the initial pilot. As mentioned earlier, reporting also provides an overview on the platform usage and potential technical problems. In many projects it is a challenge to test the implemented UC solution for all scenarios and also for the network performance that is required for a high-end communication and collaboration system. Successful projects always had proper test documentation, user acceptance testing checklists, and a documentation that lists down all the features and the core set of communication capabilities that the solution provides. It makes sense to invest time in the project to get a test team ready for platform and **user acceptance testing** (**UAT**) and to document the results in a very detailed report. For areas such as network performance, certain tools and application can benchmark the traffic and connection for audio and video communication with other communication modalities. One example here is the solution "PowerMon" by UnifySquare Inc. (http://www.unifysquare.com/), a known company in the UC space.

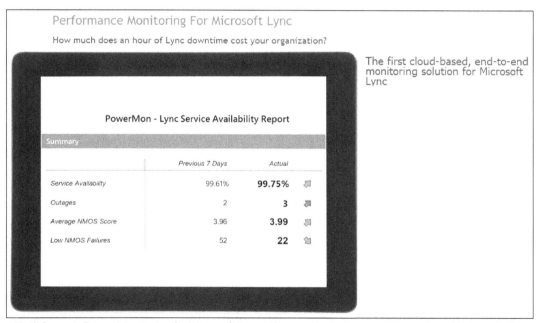

UnifySquare's Power Monitoring for Microsoft Lync – the award winning reporting and monitoring solution based on the Microsoft UC stack.

When the proof of concept and the initial deployment of the UC solution is successful, the next part of the project that is the rollout to a user group or the entire company can proceed.

Next to the deployment and the rollout of the UC solution for the entire organization, it is also important to "bring" all users onboard with the new communication and collaboration platform. Even if the project is successful in terms of implementation and rollout, it is very important to invest time and effort in the real adoption of the UC client application and dedicated real-time communication features such Enterprise Voice, video conferencing, chat, and sharing.

There are different approaches available to introduce the solution in all areas of the company and usually this is a very "hot" topic for organizations that want to migrate from legacy technology to unified communications. Some companies/projects "just" rollout the solution and let the user discover the advantages, some others provide a "one page" explanation for the users, others offer training and video/web cast sessions to understand the solution. In some cases, companies take the adoption as part of a successful project execution so they invest a lot of effort in internal adoption and incentive projects.

Some of the possible areas are listed here and can be used as a guide to drive a better UC adoption in the company. In our example, Contoso's users and power users (such as staff at the reception) supported the project with less resistance and with more enthusiasm.

- Provide new UC certified communication devices for users
- Benchmark system for users who adopt the UC solution instead of using for example legacy technology for meetings, conference calls, and so on
- Benchmark system such as "Green Points" to avoid travels and use the UC solution instead
- Development of a usage-based loyalty program that rewards the use of web conferencing
- Development of bonus program for managers who can manage a large number of successful employees with home offices
- Link the possibility of working at home with unified communications solution
- Have a group of staff who are selected to promote the UC project by sharing their experience and best practices for UC solution

It is important for the adoption to think through the preceding mentioned areas, it is also required to measure improvements for example cost savings, efficiency for communication, collaboration and the better interface to customers and business partners. The following areas can help to demonstrate the value of the UC solution in daily business:

- Development of a multimedia utility model that replaces the traditional telephone billing. This is also a good way to trace and report the "minutes" spent for all phone calls, video conferences, and so on that are made through the UC solution. This can help in a migration process to demonstrate the return on investment.

- Development of a call volume model or call charges over the existing PBX system using the SIP carrier connection model.

- Staff training, where the added value of UC technology and its operation is demonstrated.

- Development of a user model, which shows the additive load on the existing data network.

- Integration of non-PC workstations such as fax machines, lobby telephones.

- Creation of an organizational chart that defines the IT organizational structure after the rollout of the UC solution. (This often result in the a re-organization of the departments or a merger of both IT and telecommunications departments as they work more closely with each other.)

After observing the preceding points during the rollout and observation phase, we are at the end of the integration of the new unified communication technology. This does not mean that the project actually ends at this point. Real customer cases have showed that extended testing, user acceptance project, measurement of business value and potential financial benefits would still be required before the official end of the project and can also be carried on for a certain amount of time. It is important to consider how the project will be finalized and if other connected "part" projects or activities are required for the further project success. In other words, did the project meet the success criteria — the **Key Performance Indicators**'s (KPI)?

At the final project end phase, there are also other important points to consider. Most of the time, these points are forgotten due to the success of the pilot phase or little priority is placed on the project end. At the project completion, the entire project team, the integration partner (general contractor), the manufacturer, persons from the management, and selected staff from the pilot phase (for positive feedback/promote the topic) should come together for a final meeting to comment on the output and the highlights of the project.

Finally, the documentation of the entire course of the project is recommended as it serves as a reference for best practice in future projects of the company. This could be done in collaboration with the integrator or the manufacturer of the solution as a joint published reference. The document showcases not just the solution but also the innovative strength of the company in terms of new technologies and collaboration with other companies, especially with their market partners. Another benefit for the company is that by having a published reference, the supplier or system integrator might offer some other benefits such as a cost rebates, better rate for follow-up project, free infrastructure assessment, or even a reduction of the overall project costs. (In this case this should be discussed with all parties at the very beginning of the project.)

It sounds almost trite at this point, but I know from personal experience that it is often at this point of the project when payment methods of the license or service between the customers and the suppliers have not yet been resolved. This of course also includes the investment made for servers, firewall/reverse proxy (server or appliance), high available hardware to meet the SLA criteria and required certifications, the cost of purchasing audio and video conferencing devices and other areas of project cost. A conclusion of these open topics is recommended because a project must understandably always allow for buyers and suppliers to operate in a dynamic market, allowing a win-win situation.

This chapter serves as a checklist and reference for those who wish to introduce unified communications projects into their own company. Naturally this chapter is only a compact summary of the reality, where projects can develop in a variety of dynamics and conditions, so an external consultant would be necessary. Nevertheless, the example company, Contoso and its UC execution is depicted to reflect the majority of real-world projects in the unified communications and collaboration industry.

Summary

What you have learned in this chapter is how to evaluate and realize a unified communications project. It is important to think about all steps, especially whether or not you have the required support by management and all stakeholders. As mentioned before, this chapter only illustrates a compact or small part of reality. I also mentioned before the "dynamic" aspect of real projects. Every project is different. Since every unified communications project is also a change project inside the organization, some companies are very resistant against changes. Pressure for innovation on collaboration and communication might have built up over a long period of time before something can actually happen. Some projects were done due to the increasing pressure from business partners because the existing collaboration was no longer efficient or simply too expensive. There were also a few interesting experiences where change was driven by the middle-management layer and it did not get supported by stakeholders because they preferred to hold on to their legacy equipment and previous investments.

The learning point is that in most environments, innovation is possible. Of course, this may sound funny but depending on the size and culture of a company, you will realize that IT and Telecommunications related projects have their own pace and dynamism.

Indeed there are also companies/business divisions which are open for change and employees who are more than happy to drive innovation and become more competitive in the market, especially to save cost and have a better communication interface to their customers. Project managers for UC projects have to be very familiar with all needs, business requirements and internal/external company culture, and of course, potential blockers and internal politics that comes with such projects.

If all or at least most important areas are known and identified at the start of a project and if all business requirements can be resolved with the best available technology and results can be achieved or exceeded, every unified communications project should be a great success.

In the next and last chapter, we will dive into the technology part and discuss how to design, deploy, and run a great UC solution and real-time communication platform, Microsoft Lync 2013.

8
Technology Inside the Microsoft UC Platform and a Look into the Future

In the previous chapters of this book, we discussed knowledge management, collaboration management, cost optimization, communication and collaboration, as well as the general developments in unified communications.

In this chapter, we will look from a technological point at Microsoft's current unified communications solution, Lync Server, in detail. It is important to highlight that Microsoft offers detailed documentation and online curriculums for Lync 2013 deployment design, implementation, and troubleshooting. It should be noted that technology is always a snapshot as it is always rapidly changing and evolving within a short period of time. However, this chapter will provide a good high-level overview of the technology of Lync 2013, and the design and installation of this great new version.

Microsoft Lync Server 2013

Lync Server 2013 is Microsoft's latest solution for real-time communication and it represents the next technological step to make communication between people and businesses easier and efficient. Lync Server 2013 is the next generation of Lync Server 2010 and Office Communications Server 2007 R2. It has both platform enhancements as well as new features such as the ability to dial-in audio conferencing, desktop sharing from any workstation, persistent chat (Group Chat) integration, and also the availability of Lync "mobile" for mobile device platforms such as Windows 8 and Windows 8 RT, Apple IOS, Google Android, BlackBerry, and many others.

Like almost every Microsoft product, Lync Server 2013 has a client-server architecture and thus it has various client integrations and access options. This means that the end user has many enhanced and new ways of communication and collaboration from anywhere and at any time. Integrated together with Microsoft Office, SharePoint, Microsoft Dynamics/CRM, Windows Phone, Exchange Server, and many other solutions, Lync Server 2013 offers a broad set of extensibility and implementation scenarios. Lync 2013 also integrates closely with traditional **private branch exchange (PBX)** systems, which enables telephony integration from any line of businesses and third-party applications to allow us to answer incoming calls on Lync instead of using the traditional desktop telephone. Lync 2013 also offers, for the first time, integration not only for an On-Premise model but also for a hybrid installation with Microsoft cloud solution, Office 365 and Lync online.

Before the Lync Server 2013 can be integrated within the company's IT backend systems, it is important to question which features are needed. So devising a plan to determine whether features such as **instant messaging (IM)**, presence integration, VoIP telephony, video conferencing, audio conferencing, desktop sharing, and Group Chat are to be used in the company or by external users on the Internet is necessary.

The Lync Server 2013 can offer most of the communication options needed in **business-to-business (B2B)** cooperation or collaboration of distributed teams within a company to achieve efficiency as well as sustainable cost optimization. Therefore, we need detailed planning and collection of functional requirements, technical integration considerations, or any other integration requirements as desired with other applications such as CRM, SharePoint, or SAP. This is an important planning step in a UC project.

Lync topology planning

Microsoft provides several tools to help in planning and designing the Lync Server environment. The Lync Server Planning Tool can be used by IT teams and Lync architects to answer topology-related questions such as how many Enterprise Voice users are needed, whether Lync needs to be integrated as a high-availability solution or features like Federation, mobile access, reporting, and monitoring are required. This Planning Tool features a question and answer type graphical interface which gathers information about your setup to generate a reference topology according to the Lync Server guidelines and best practices for you. It is also possible to generate several deployment options that you can use to make your final topology design decision. Another benefit is that all these deployment options come with detailed Lync configuration and implementation instructions.

Additionally, this tool is able to display a global view of the geographic location of all the servers, client computers, and so on that is in the entire company's network, inclusive of all the branch offices in every location. Note that running the Planning Tool does not automatically bind a specific deployment or initiate any setup processes for you. Instead, once your draft implementation is ready for deployment, the Implementation team is able to use the Lync Topology Builder in the Planning Tool to create the "master plan", which is a diagram of the finalized implemented deployment.

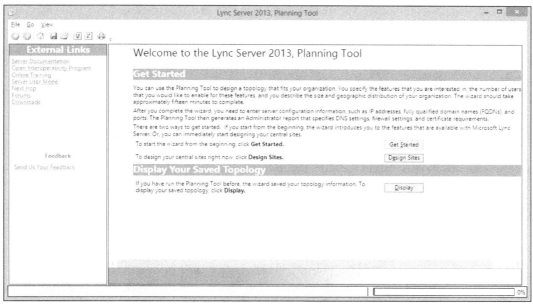

The Lync Server 2013 Planning Tool user interface

 Lync 2013 Planning Tool download: `http://www.microsoft.com/en-us/download/details.aspx?id=36823`.

Migrating from another Lync or OCS topology

A migration process is always needed because it is impossible to "update" an existing Lync or OCS topology. When migrating from an existing Lync Server 2010 or Office Communications Server 2007 R2 environment to the new Lync 2013, Microsoft offers step-by-step instructions in the technical design documentation to implement the new Lync infrastructure into the company's environment and then migrate every user from the old into the new topology before the "old" environment is decommissioned. Microsoft offers a couple of different ways to carry out a migration:

- **Side-by-side migration**: This is a common migration type for Lync projects. In a side-by-side migration, Lync 2013 is placed and deployed in an existing Lync 2010 or Office Communications Server 2007 R2 environment. In this case, all configurations such as policies, voice routes, and so on and all operations are transferred from the previous Lync 2010 environment to the new Lync 2013 environment. However, this method requires additional server hardware, certificates, potential voice gateways, and other software because a separate configuration (such as different server names) in the company's IT environment needs to be set up.

- **Coexistence with Lync Server 2013 and previous versions**: In this scenario, Lync Server 2013 can coexist with other versions like Lync Server 2010 or even with the previous Office Communications Server 2007 R2 in the same environment. This is useful when Lync 2013 is deployed and the previous versions of Lync need to be decommissioned after a certain period of coexistence. In certain environments, this kind of installation can be a requirement. However, it is important to understand limitations of such a migration. For example, mixed version routing for Lync clients and running all three versions at the same time is not supported in the same environment.

Creating a new Lync topology

Topology Builder is the main tool that is utilized for the planning of the Lync topology and to author how the Lync environment will look like so that the different components can be deployed. The administrator first uses the Topology Builder as the visual interface to set up and configure the Lync Servers. Once the initial set up process is done, the Topology Builder is used to validate the new topology. Once the validation is successful, this topology can then be published into the **Central Management Store** (**CMS**). Lync Servers, both physical and virtual, then installs itself based on the role assigned to it that depends on the published topology stored in the CMS. This publishing process ensures that only a validated published topology can be deployed into the Lync Server.

At this point, you may have noticed that it is possible to skip the Planning Tool and go straight into the Topology Builder for the creation, validation, publication, and deployment of the design to the Lync Servers. The following screenshot shows the deployment wizard for the installation of Topology Builder and Lync Server 2013:

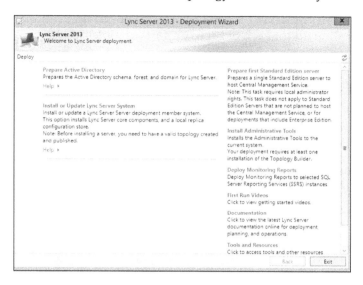

The following screenshot shows the configuration of Lync Server environment through the Topology Builder:

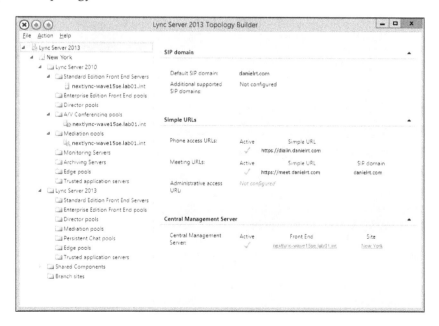

At this point it is important to mention that for the installation of Topology Builder and Lync 2013, it is necessary to install the administrative tools of Lync 2013 first.

It is also important to have a detailed knowledge of how Lync 2013 works, what kind of server roles are required, an understanding of Active Directory and networking infrastructure before embarking on any planning and set up actions. Hence, I have included information about each of these important topics here.

Server roles and editions

A Lync Server is made up of several main server roles. Based on the Lync 2013 topology, each of these servers has a defined set of functionalities which we will go into more detail later. In a typical Lync topology, we have the following server roles:

- Front End Server
- Back End Server (Microsoft SQL)
- Edge Server
- Mediation Server
- Director Server
- Persistent Chat Server (formerly Group Chat Servers)

 A full list of functionalities of all Lync 2013 server components can be found on the following Microsoft website: `http://technet.microsoft.com/en-us/library/gg398536(v=ocs.15).aspx`.

Microsoft offers two different versions of the Lync Server 2013: the Lync Standard Edition and Lync Enterprise Edition. It is important to select the correct version based on your company's needs. There are also On-Premise and cloud-based versions, we will talk about each of these versions in more detail later.

Lync Standard Edition

The Standard version is designed for small organizations (up to 5,000 users in the company) and could also be used to create pilot projects in larger organizations. The Standard Edition server enables IM, presence, conferencing, and Enterprise Voice, all integrated into one single Lync server.

Since it is possible to run this version on a single server, complete with many of the features of the Lync Server and all its necessary databases, it is not a true high-availability solution. Hence, this standard version has a lower cost compared to the Enterprise edition.

Lync Enterprise Edition

The Enterprise Edition is usually the best choice for projects where up to 100,000 users or more need to be part of the Lync Server environment. Similar to previous versions of Lync, the Front End Server is still at the "core" in the Lync 2013 topology and it runs many of the basic functions of the Lync Server.

Since it is possible to designate server roles on separate servers and to have a multiserver model, this allows for higher performance, better reliability, and higher availability.

At this point, let us take a closer look at the main Lync Server considerations, roles, and its functionalities.

Lync Server considerations, roles, and functionalities

In the implementation of the Lync server roles, scalability and high availability are important considerations. It is recommended to dedicate each pool of multiple servers to run a single server role. To fully utilize the server pools, a load balancer can be used to help spread the traffic and determine the role each pool of servers takes on. The Lync Server supports both, **Domain Name System** (**DNS**) load balancing and hardware load balancing. Currently, the hardware load balancer is the most common option but it is also the most expensive.

Front End Server

The Front End Server is the "core" server in the Lync topology as it runs most of the basic communication and collaboration features. The Front End Server is used in the integration of all basic features such as IM, presence information, address book synchronization with e-mail service (for example, Exchange Server) in the company, audio and video conferencing in the corporate network, UC workflow integration, and so on.

The Front End Server includes the following:

- User registration
- User authentication
- Presence information and contact information store
- Address book services and distribution list expansion
- IM functionality, including multiparty IM conferences

- Web conferencing, PSTN dial-in conferencing, and A/V conferencing (if deployed)

- Application hosting, for applications included with Lync Server (for example, Conferencing Attendant and Response Group application), and third-party applications

- Monitoring and reporting, used in the collection of usage information in the form of **call detail records (CDRs)** and **call error records (CERs)**, to provide metrics about the **Quality of Experience (QoE)**of the media (audio and video) traversing your network for both Enterprise Voice calls, A/V conferences, and other P2P conversations

- Web components to supported web-based tasks such as web scheduler and join launcher

- Archiving, to archive IM communications and meeting content for compliance reasons

- Persistent Chat Web Services for Chat Room Management and Persistent Chat Web Services for File Upload/Download

Back End Server

The Back End Server exists as a dedicated SQL server in the Enterprise Edition, while it is included as a single server in the Standard Edition together with the SQL Express version.

The Back End Servers act as backup storage for all the users and conference data that are stored in the Front End Servers. They also function as primary storages for other databases like the Response Group database. In terms of technology, these Back End Servers run on Microsoft SQL Server and use SQL Server mirroring for the Front End Servers to create a high-availability environment.

Edge Server

The Edge Server is like the edge separating your organization and users outside the organization. Communication and collaboration with external users, who are outside the company and the organization's firewall environment is made possible with the Edge Server. The Edge Server is always located in the DMZ for security reasons and also requires multiple network interfaces pointing to the "external" and "internal" side of the Lync environment.

Who are the external users? External users include the organization's own users who are currently working offsite, users from federated partner organizations, and any other users who are invited to join conferences hosted on your Lync Server deployment. Edge Server enables connectivity to public IM connectivity services, including Windows Live/ Skype, AOL, Yahoo!, and Google Talk.

Important information for Public Internet Connectivity (PIC)

The integration with available services like Windows Live, AOL, and so on can change based on updates for the Lync 2013 or if Microsoft as the design manufacturer has decided to add/remove certain services. This change is ongoing as new public communication services are constantly entering the market and need to be able to establish a connection to certain communication modalities in Lync 2013 and other future versions.

Lync on mobile devices is also enabled through this Edge Server. The mobility feature in Lync supports many popular mobile platforms/brands such as Apple iOS, Android, Windows, and Nokia mobile devices. You are able to send and receive instant messages and view contacts and presence information on your mobile devices. Certain Enterprise Voice features such as click to join a conference, call via work, single number reach, voicemail, and missed calls are also made available. A relatively new feature is the ability to make voice calls and video conferences from mobile devices that are on the current main platforms such as Windows (Microsoft), iOS (Apple), Android (Google), and Symbian (Nokia). For mobile devices that do not support applications running in the background, the push notification feature is also supported within this feature.

The Edge Server also includes a fully integrated **Extensible Messaging and Presence Protocol (XMPP)** proxy. Together with the XMPP gateway included on Front End Servers, these XMPP components work together to enable Lync Server 2013 users to add contacts from XMPP-based partners (such as Google Talk or any other third-party services) to display availability/presence information and to allow IM.

Mediation Server

The Mediation Server is needed in the implementation of Enterprise Voice and dial-in conferencing features. It is responsible for signal translation and acts as the media between the **public switched telephone network (PSTN)** gateway, IP-PBX, or a **Session Initiation Protocol (SIP)** trunk and your internal Lync Server infrastructure.

For deployment consideration, the Mediation Server has the option to be collocated on the same server as the Front End Server (similar to the setup in Lync 2013 Standard Edition), or be configured as a standalone Mediation Server pool. The reason for collocation is to reduce the amount of physical or virtual servers that are required for certain deployment options.

Director Server

The Director Server acts as the security guard for your Lync configuration. It secures your internal servers from attacks by authenticating all Lync Server users and any requests from external users, before sending them to the internal servers. Therefore, before requests are sent to the Front End Server to allow communication and collaboration with external users, they must first go through the Director Server. This keeps the Front End Servers which contain the fundamental setup information and important databases safe from unauthorized external access. One important thing to note is that the Director Server under Lync 2013 is deemphasized and its importance has diminished since several functions can be performed by the FE pool as well.

Group Chat Server(s)

Group Chat is a great option for deploying Persistent Chat inside the company. Unfortunately, it is not one of the "popular" services in Lync 2010. This is, perhaps, due to the need to integrate two separate clients in Lync 2010 and their IT departments did not want to integrate two separate clients for their end users. However, Group Chat in Lync 2013 is now integrated in one single client, so it is definitely interesting to think about this in your deployment.

Group Chat Servers host the Persistent Chat feature for Lync. What it allows is multiparty, topic-based conversations that last over a long period of time. Any authorized user can join the chat and be able to view past comments from other users while the user is not online.

To implement Persistent Chat (formerly known as Group Chat) in the Lync 2013 environment, some additional servers and roles are required:

- Persistent Chat Front End Server
- Persistent Chat Compliance Store (Persistent Chat Compliance Back End Server)
- Persistent Chat Store (Persistent Chat Back End Server)

The Persistent Chat Front End Server runs the Persistent Chat service. The Persistent Chat Back End Server acts as the database to store chat history data, chat room category information, and so on. The optional Persistent Chat Compliance Back End Server is for compliance purposes so it can store chat content and other necessary compliance events.

Servers running Lync Server Standard Edition can run the Persistent Chat collocated on the same server as the Front End Server. In the Enterprise Edition, the Group Chat Server needs to be on a different server as the Front End Server.

Enterprise Voice with Lync 2013 Standard Edition

The following diagram depicts topology of the new Lync Server 2013 with limited high availability. In this scenario Lync 2013 is installed on a single Front End Server, single Edge Server, and the required backend database (SQL Express for the Standard Edition) as part of the Lync Standard Edition. The Lync Standard Edition with the integrated (collocated) Mediation Server can also be integrated with the PSTN network by a VoIP Gateway, Direct SIP, or Lync certified PBX, the diagram illustrates a full-featured (all communication modalities) UC environment. In our example, we assume that the Mediation Server is collocated together with the Front End Server.

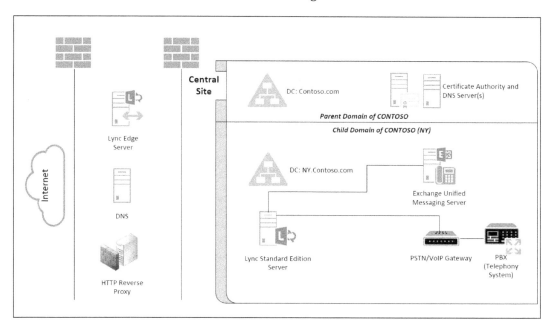

The following diagram depicts the topology of the new Lync Server 2013 with high availability and a single data center. Compared to the Lync Server Standard Edition, the Enterprise Edition offers the option to set up multiple servers for higher availability or to separate the workload between multiple servers in the Lync Enterprise pool for all main server roles. The diagram shows an optimal environment with two Lync Front End servers, Edge Servers, Director Servers, Persistent Chat Servers (Group Chat), and Mediation Servers for the implementation of Enterprise Voice with dedicated VoIP gateways and PBX integration. The Edge Servers, Front End Servers, Director Servers, and SQL Servers can be installed as high-availability "pool" of servers. Other servers such as the Mediation, Monitoring, and Persistent Chat servers need to be installed in multiple ways with the same configuration — in terms of high availability.

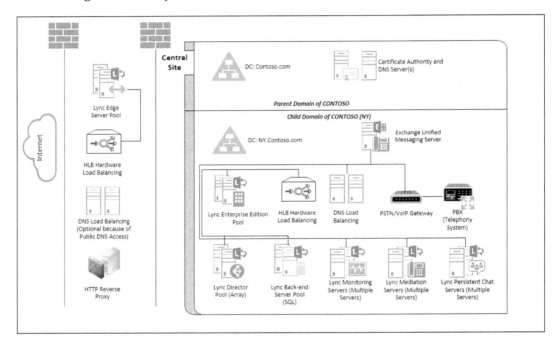

The following image shows the topology of the new Lync Server 2013 with high availability and "failover" data center — A. Next to the high-availability infrastructure in Central Site A, there are two company branch sites which are part of the Lync environment. As all the server roles in Central Site A have redundant servers, users in Branch Site 1 and Branch Site 2 would benefit from this high service level in case of a network, server, or Lync outage.

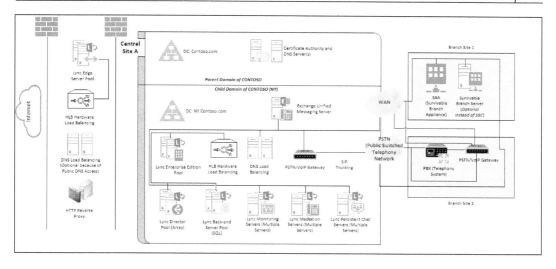

The following image shows the topology of the new Lync Server 2013 with high availability and "failover" data center — B. Central Site A integrates two Branch Sites into the deployment. Central Site B illustrates the integration of Branch Site 3 inclusive of the availability of Enterprise Voice.

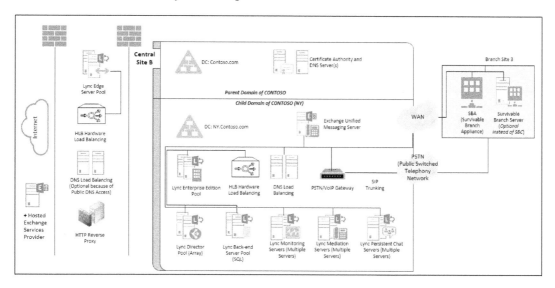

Branch Site with Lync 2013

One of the major new features available in Microsoft's version of the Office Communications Server 2007 R2 and newer versions is the integration of branch-office scenarios. This function can be activated to enable a reliable branch office installation with the Lync Server 2013 topology. A branch office is a location (other than the main office), where business is conducted. Usually a branch office is a smaller office as compared to the main office and it needs some kind of IT infrastructure. Lync 2013 supports branch office installation in several different ways to extend communication and collaboration modalities to other office locations and to build a high-availablility infrastructure as well as in case of an interruption in the connectivity to the main office.

The installation of Lync 2013 with a branch site offers the capability to make and receive phone calls at the branch site even when the central site hosting the "main" Lync 2013 environment is temporarily unavailable.

For the branch to provide calls to and from the PSTN, it usually has the following:

- An existing voice infrastructure with a PBX
- A SIP trunk
- A PSTN gateway and possibly a Meditation Server
- A Survivable Branch Appliance
- A Survivable Branch Server

This branch-office function using Lync Server branch office technology can be integrated on a Windows server or on a dedicated appliance. Dialogic, AudioCodes, Ferrari electronic, HP, Cisco, and other certified manufacturers offer these appliances as part of their product lines.

The decision to use a Survivable Branch Appliance or a dedicated Lync Survivable Branch Server depends on the number of users in the branch site. If you have a user range of 25 to a maximum of 1,000 users, it is recommended to choose the Survivable Branch Appliance and for a user range of 1,000 to 5,000, it is recommended to use the Survivable Branch Server.

An example of a possible branch-office integration of Lync Server 2013 is illustrated in the following diagram. For more information, refer to the Microsoft white papers and the Microsoft TechNet Web portal at the following URLs:

`http://technet.microsoft.com/en-us/library/gg425833(v=ocs.15)` and
`http://technet.microsoft.com/en-us/library/gg398234.aspx`

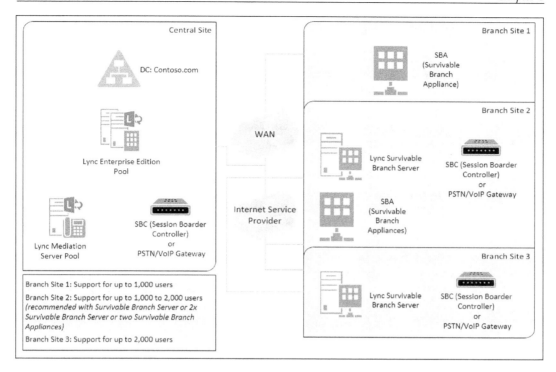

Operation system and virtualization

For Lync Server 2013, the basic requirement for the operating system platform is Windows Server 2008 R2 with Service Pack 1 or Windows Server 2012. The use of workloads in virtual environments for cost-efficient and energy-saving operations as well as the ability to combine various virtualization technologies from any manufacturer is new to Lync. As we already know, a high-availability environment can be created in the Enterprise Edition of the Lync Server 2013 and with virtualization, it can be used to create another version of this high-availability infrastructure to reduce the hardware implementation cost for Lync.

Lync Server 2013 supports all Lync Server workloads in virtualization topologies

Virtualization of all Lync Server workloads is fully supported in Lync Server 2013 with some differences in the Standard and Enterprise version. These includes the most commonly used functionalities such as IM and presence, conferencing, Enterprise Voice, monitoring, archiving, and Persistent Chat. However, these virtualized servers must run on Windows Server 2012 or Windows Server 2008 R2—Service Pack 1 Hyper-V or VMWare vSphere 5 or higher. A combination of both physical and virtual servers in the same pool is not supported within the Lync topology. What is supported today allows you to implement, for example, the Lync 2013 servers into a virtual environment but the SQL Server is considered a separate role from the Lync 2013 pool. The SQL Server can be virtualized or physical no matter what your choice of Lync 2013 deployment is. It is important to note that you should not implement other applications and workloads on the SQL Server, especially if it is virtualized. However, an important consideration is the real-time data requirement between the Front End Servers which functions as the Lync control center and the Back End Servers which function as the database in the Lync topology. Hence, for better performance, it is often better to have a physical system instead of a virtual system for the all Back End Servers.

> More information about VMWare vSphere 5 virtualization:
> `http://www.vmware.com/products/datacenter-virtualization/vsphere/overview.html?src=WWW_BestMatch_US#utm_source=WWW_BestMatch_US&utm_medium=src&utm_campaign=src-tagged-url`.

It is a requirement that every Lync Server pool should provide the same level of performance because correct server sizing dictates the capacity that ultimately determines the ability to support the expected load in the event of an outage. In other words, when working with virtualization, it is necessary to verify that each pool on a virtual server (for example, Front End Server) has the same level of performance, in the event that a Lync Server role gets moved to another host sever (for example, Hyper-V/Windows Server). It is also important to ensure that performance will not be reduced at this point, otherwise users may complain about the differences in their user experience.

Lync Server also supports the use of virtual clustered storage. However, live migration (and other types of migration) of virtual servers running Lync Server is currently not supported by Microsoft. SQL clustering is not supported in both physical and virtual Lync environments.

The following UC scenarios are supported in virtual or physical environments and installations:

	Physical Hardware	Virtualized Hardware
Lync Enterprise Edition		
Audio-Video conferencing pool	x	x
Director Pool	x	x
Archiving/Monitor-Server	x	x
Mediation Server	x	x
Edge Server	x	x
SQL Back-End Server	x	x
Lync Standard Edition		
Lync Standard Edition Server (all workloads)	x	x
Edge Server	x	x

Network performance for communication and collaboration

The next important topic to consider is the company's network performance. Whether Lync deployed on physical or virtual servers affects the overall network performance. As mentioned earlier, the Lync Server is responsible for real-time communications so it requires a fast and efficient network. If a data packet is delayed by just a few milliseconds, it would appear to the users as an audio glitch, a voice delay, or a frozen video.

Here are some tips to configure the company's network to improve the performance of Lync:

- Have at least one dedicated network adapter to the servers running Lync Server roles. Sharing of a network adapter with the Windows Server (or host) or **storage area network (SAN)** is not recommended as it may result in irregularities with the "voice data" if Lync Front End Server or Mediation Server used shared network interfaces.

- Expect a peak network utilization greater than 500 Mbps, including media data, in the Lync Server.

- Ensure that the network adapter of the servers is able to handle the traffic of the Lync Server media workloads, especially when you have multiple virtual guest servers running on a single host server. Consider using a high-speed network adapter (perhaps a 10 GbE) or multiple network adapters using link aggregation. Microsoft also recommends the network adapters to be configured for NIC-teaming to provide a better high-availability solution on the network side. Network adapter teaming, also known as **Network Interface Card (NIC)**teaming is a great Windows Server 2012 feature and can be used for Lync 2010 and also Lync 2013 deployments.

- Utilize the **Single Root I/O Virtualization (SR-IOV)** capabilities of Windows Server 2012 Hyper-V for best performance as it is able to increase network throughput, reduce network latency, and reduce host CPU overhead for network traffic processing. What SR-IOV does is allow the virtual function of a physical network adapter to be assigned directly to a virtual machine. To enable SR-IOV in your configuration, ensure that your host server has a BIOS that supports SR-IOV and the network adapters also support SR-IOV.

- Enable **virtual LAN (VLAN)** tagging on the network adapter and implement multiple VLANs on the virtual servers to optimize network traffic.

- Implement multipath I/O (MPIO) to your backend database.

For more information on Network Adapter Teaming, visit the Microsoft website: http://support.microsoft.com/kb/2478464?wa=wsignin1.0.

A complete table on Network Ports can be accessed on the Microsoft website: http://technet.microsoft.com/en-us/library/gg425882.aspx and http://technet.microsoft.com/en-us/library/gg398833.aspx.

Network port and security in Lync 2013

Similar to the previous versions of Lync 2010 or Office Communications Server 2007 R2, it is necessary to configure the ports for **Audio/Video (A/V)** communication, authentication, registration, and any other required scenarios for your topology. Due to the nature of protocols and how clients and servers use the protocols in Lync 2013, this section deserves special attention.

A common scenario in most complex environments is that Lync 2013 clients or servers are not able to communicate with each other. The most common reasons for such failures are certificates, DNS, or simply configuration issues. Another possible reason for this failure is not having the correct ports enabled for the communication and collaboration with Lync 2013.

Ports and protocols for internal servers

The following table shows the required server ports settings (by server role) for all communication and collaboration scenarios:

Server role	Service name	Port	Protocol
All Servers	SQL Browser	1434	UDP
Front End Servers	Lync Server Front-End service	5060	TCP
Front End Servers	Lync Server Front-End service	5061	TCP (TLS)
Front End Servers	Lync Server Front-End service	444	HTTPS TCP
Front End Servers	Lync Server Front-End service	135	DCOM and remote procedure call (RPC)
Front End Servers	Lync Server IM Conferencing service	5062	TCP
Front End Servers	Lync Server Web Conferencing service	8057	TCP (TLS)
Front End Servers	Lync Server Web Conferencing Compatibility service	8058	TCP (TLS)
Front End Servers	Lync Server Audio/Video Conferencing service	5063	TCP
Front End Servers	Lync Server Audio/Video Conferencing service	57501-65335	TCP/UDP
Front End Servers	Lync Server Web Compatibility service	80	HTTP
Front End Servers	Lync Server Web Compatibility service	443	HTTPS
Front End Servers	Lync Server Web Compatibility service	8080	TCP and HTTP
Front End Servers	Web server component	4443	HTTPS
Front End Servers	Web server component	8060	TCP (MTLS)
Front End Servers	Web server component	8061	TCP (MTLS)
Front End Servers	Mobility Services component	5086	TCP (MTLS)
Front End Servers	Mobility Services component	5087	TCP (MTLS)
Front End Servers	Mobility Services component	443	HTTPS

Server role	Service name	Port	Protocol
Front End Servers	Lync Server Conferencing Attendant service (dial-in conferencing)	5064	TCP
Front End Servers	Lync Server Conferencing Attendant service (dial-in conferencing)	5072	TCP
Front End Servers that also run a Collocated Mediation Server	Lync Server Mediation service	5070	TCP
Front End Servers that also run a Collocated Mediation Server	Lync Server Mediation service	5067	TCP (TLS)
Front End Servers that also run a Collocated Mediation Server	Lync Server Mediation service	5068	TCP
Front End Servers that also run a Collocated Mediation Server	Lync Server Mediation service	5081	TCP
Front End Servers that also run a Collocated Mediation Server	Lync Server Mediation service	5082	TCP (TLS)
Front End Servers	Lync Server Application Sharing service	5065	TCP
Front End Servers	Lync Server Application Sharing service	49152-65335	TCP
Front End Servers	Lync Server Conferencing Announcement service	5073	TCP
Front End Servers	Lync Server Call Park service	5075	TCP
Front End Servers	Lync Server Audio Test service	5076	TCP
Front End Servers	Not applicable	5066	TCP
Front End Servers	Lync Server Response Group service	5071	TCP
Front End Servers	Lync Server Response Group service	8404	TCP (MTLS)

Server role	Service name	Port	Protocol
Front End Servers	Lync Server Bandwidth Policy Service	5080	TCP
Front End Servers	Lync Server Bandwidth Policy Service	448	TCP
Front End Servers where the Central Management store resides	Lync Server Master Replicator Agent service	445	TCP
All Servers	SQL Browser	1434	UDP
All internal servers	Various	49152-57500	TCP/UDP
Directors	Lync Server Front End service	5060	TCP
Directors	Lync Server Front End service	444	HTTPS TCP
Directors	Lync Server Web Compatibility service	80	TCP
Directors	Lync Server Web Compatibility service	443	HTTPS
Directors	Lync Server Front End service	5061	TCP
Mediation Servers	Lync Server Mediation service	5070	TCP
Mediation Servers	Lync Server Mediation service	5067	TCP (TLS)
Mediation Servers	Lync Server Mediation service	5068	TCP
Mediation Servers	Lync Server Mediation service	5070	TCP (MTLS)
Persistent Chat Front End Server	Persistent Chat SIP	5041	TCP (MTLS)
Persistent Chat Front End Server	Persistent Chat Windows Communication Foundation (WCF)	881	TCP (TLS) and TCP (MTLS)
Persistent Chat Front End Server	Persistent Chat File Transfer Service	443	TCP (TLS)

A complete table of network ports can be accessed on the Microsoft website: http://technet.microsoft.com/en-us/library/gg425882.aspx and http://technet.microsoft.com/en-us/library/gg398833.aspx.

The following table shows the hardware load balancer ports when using only hardware load balancing (not DNS load balancing):

Load balancer	Port	Protocol
Front End Server load balancer	5061	TCP (TLS)
Front End Server load balancer	444	HTTPS
Front End Server load balancer	135	DCOM and remote procedure call (RPC)
Front End Server load balancer	80	HTTP
Front End Server load balancer	8080	TCP carries out client and device retrieval of root certificates from Front End Server, and clients and devices are authenticated by NTLM
Front End Server load balancer	443	HTTPS
Front End Server load balancer	4443	HTTPS (from reverse proxy)
Front End Server load balancer	5072	TCP
Front End Server load balancer	5073	TCP
Front End Server load balancer	5075	TCP
Front End Server load balancer	5076	TCP
Front End Server load balancer	5071	TCP
Front End Server load balancer	5080	TCP
Front End Server load balancer	448	TCP
Mediation Server load balancer	5070	TCP
Front End Server load balancer (if the pool also runs Mediation Server)	5070	TCP
Director load balancer	443	HTTPS
Director load balancer	444	HTTPS
Director load balancer	5061	TCP
Director load balancer	4443	HTTPS (from reverse proxy)

The following table shows the hardware load balancer ports when using DNS load balancing:

Load balancer	Port	Protocol
Front End Server load balancer	80	HTTP
Front End Server load balancer	443	HTTPS
Front End Server load balancer	8080	TCP carried out client and device retrieval of root certificates from Front End Server, and clients and devices authenticated by NTLM
Front End Server load balancer	4443	HTTPS (from reverse proxy)
Director load balancer	443	HTTPS
Director load balancer	444	HTTPS
Director load balancer	4443	HTTPS (from reverse proxy)

The following table shows the required client ports:

Component	Port	Protocol
Clients	67/68	DHCP
Clients	443	TCP (TLS)
Clients	443	TCP (PSOM/TLS)
Clients	443	TCP (STUN/MSTURN)
Clients	3478	UDP (STUN/MSTURN)
Clients	5061	TCP (MTLS)
Clients	6891-6901	TCP
Clients	6891-6901	TCP
Clients	1024-65535 *	TCP/UDP
Clients	1024-65535 *	TCP/UDP
Clients	1024-65535 *	TCP
Clients	1024-65535 *	TCP

Component	Port	Protocol
Aastra 6721ip common area phone	67/68	DHCP
Aastra 6725ip desk phone		
HP 4110 IP Phone (common area phone)		
HP 4120 IP Phone (desk phone)		
Polycom CX500 IP common area phone		
Polycom CX600 IP desk phone		
Polycom CX700 IP desk phone		
Polycom CX3000 IP conference phone		

External A/V firewall and port requirements

For destination ports only, the Audio/Video requirements are:

Source IP	Destination IP	Destination Port
A/V Edge service interface	Any	TCP 443
A/V Edge service interface	Any	UDP 3478
Any	A/V Edge service interface	TCP 443
Any	A/V Edge service interface	UDP 3478

For both inbound and outbound firewall rule definitions, the Audio/Video requirements are:

Source IP	Destination IP	Source Port	Destination Port
A/V Edge service interface	Any	TCP 50,000-59,999	TCP 443
A/V Edge service interface	Any	UDP 3478	UDP 3478
Any	A/V Edge service interface	Any	TCP 443
Any	A/V Edge service interface	Any	UDP 3478

Administration of a Lync Server topology

Administration is performed through two different paths based on PowerShell and web-based GUI (Lync Control Panel requires Microsoft Silverlight browser plug-in version 4.0.50524.0 or higher). With the integration of PowerShell in Lync Server 2013, every day administrative tasks such as user and system configurations, or even special configurations such as branch-office integration and call admission control can be done using PowerShell. Other administrative operations such as an adaptation for limited requests and activities can be managed using the web-based GUI. The following screenshot shows the Lync 2013 Control Panel:

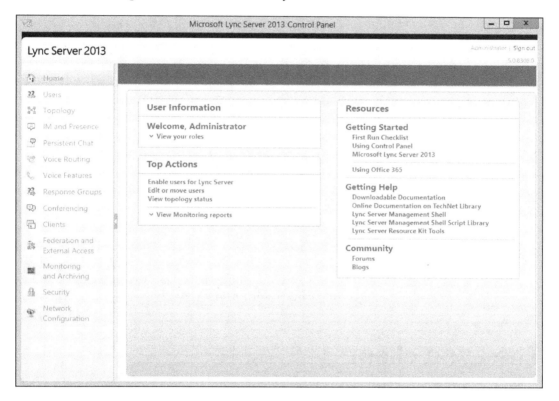

The following screenshot shows the page when the **Clients** option is selected:

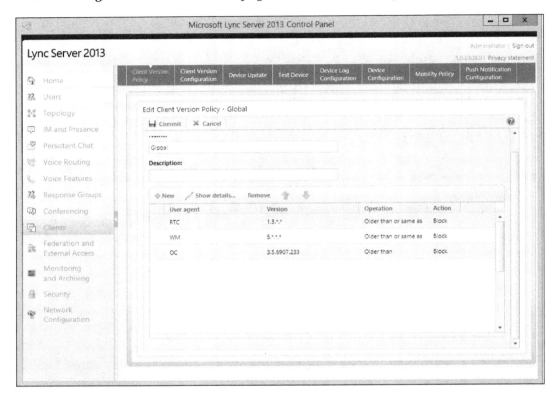

 Lync Control Panel is currently supported on browsers that allow/support the required Microsoft Silverlight plugin.

The Lync client

After having talked about an overview of the Lync Server 2013 server news and facts, let us move on to the Lync client. The Lync client 2013 can be deployed in several different ways. Lync 2013 offers a broad set of different install packages such as for a computer-installed client software installation, web-based clients, and also for mobile devices. Although this provides high accessibility for the users as Lync can be accessed from many devices, the selection of the appropriate Lync 2013 client for the environment would depend on usage objectives and user/client scenarios.

Lync 2013 offers a fully-featured client that provides access to many known and also brand new features such as presence integration, IM, Audio/Video communication, and Persistent Chat/Group Chat integration (a new feature), tabbed conversations (a new feature), multiparty video (a new feature), video preview, integration of Microsoft OneNote (a new feature) for meeting notes, and many more. Lync 2013 also has a complete user interface redesign from the previous Lync 2010 release.

Features available in the Lync 2013 client family

The following features are available in the Lync 2013 client family:

- **Online Meeting Add-in**: The Online Meeting Add-in supports the management of "online" meetings within Microsoft Outlook and is part of the typical setup of Lync 2013. This new version of the Online Meeting Add-in replaced older versions such as the Live Meeting 2007 add-in with many new meeting features (for example, setting up meeting lobby's, announcement service, and so on).

- **Lync Web App**: This powerful browser integrated app allows a user who does not have Lync 2013 installed on the computer to join a Lync meeting with a rich set of Lync functionalities. Through this web app, they are able to have audio, video, sharing, and instant messaging conversations with a Lync-based user. Due to such enhancements in this web app, the Lync 2010 Attendee client is no longer available in Lync 2013.

- **Lync Web Scheduler**: This is a web-based option for Lync users who do not have Microsoft Outlook or are on an operating system which is not supported by the Lync clients to schedule and manage meetings.

- **Lync 2013 Basic Client**: The Lync 2013 Basic client is available for users or customers who have a licensed, On-Premise version of Lync 2013 and for customers who are using Lync in the cloud through the Microsoft Office 365 offering. The Lync Basic client includes the following feature set, presence integration (enhanced presence), IM, Lync meetings, and basic voice functionality. The Lync Basic client, however, does not offer multiparty video, Microsoft OneNote integration, virtual desktop infrastructure support, skill search, Enterprise Voice features, advanced call handling (for example: Team Call function), and recording of meetings.

- **Lync Windows Store app (A touch-based app)**: The Lync Windows Store app, previously known as the Windows "Metro" app, is a new addition to the family of Lync clients. With this touch-optimized app, it is possible to use the rich features of Lync for collaboration and communication on the new Windows 8 Pro and RT devices.

- **Mobile clients**: With the growth of mobile devices and platforms, Microsoft also offers the Lync 2013 client integration across many different platforms. This is definitely a huge advantage as compared to its predecessors, Lync 2010 and Office Communications Sever 2007 R2, which offered only a very limited availability for mobile platforms. The currently supported platforms are Windows Phone, iPhone, iPad, Android, Blackberry, and Nokia Symbian. However, the feature set of the Lync 2013 can be slightly different on the different mobile platforms.

A complete list and comparison of all Lync clients and features can be found on the Microsoft TechNet web page, `http://technet.microsoft.com/en-us/library/gg425836.aspx`. Do take time to look at the following topics on the TechNet page:

- Enhanced support for presence
- Contacts and support for contact groups
- Support for instant messaging
- Support for conferencing
- Support for telephony
- Support for external users
- Support for archiving and compliance

The following main features and capability differences of all current mobile client versions can be found on TechNet at `http://technet.microsoft.com/en-us/library/hh691004.aspx`:

- Sign-in and push notifications
- Enhanced presence support in Lync mobile clients
- Contacts and contact groups support
- Instant messaging support
- Conferencing support
- Telephony support
- External user support

Lync 2013 in contact center deployments

Most of the deployment scenarios for Lync 2013 are for medium or enterprise installations. In such deployments, usually, a complete or a subset of the available communication and collaboration modalities are integrated.

Let us evaluate a special scenario where Lync 2013 is deployed in a contact center and customer care environment. Yes, you can trust Lync. It can also be used in contact center deployments but it is very important to think about how you want to deliver certain communication and collaboration scenarios.

The flexibility of Lync 2013 allows it to be utilized in many different ways and this makes it an extremely valuable solution for contact center projects. Lync 2013 offers a broad set of API's for the custom development of Lync so that it can be used in a contact center environment: The Lync 2013 Managed API, unified communications Web API, and unified communications Managed API 4.0 provide a set of development tools and interfaces to allow custom development of contact center scenarios like customer-support agent interactions, contact center agents-supervisor interactions, and so on, by extending the current Lync 2013 functionalities. There are many useful examples found on the Microsoft TechNet portal/forum which further explains how to build contact center "apps" and extensions for Lync 2013.

An example of a possible integration and custom development scenario is the implementation of a web chat solution where customers can start an IM conversation with an available support agent (with presence information displayed) and Lync is used as the communication interface with the customer.

Another example is to integrate a "call back" or "schedule a call" function on a web page where customers can initiate a call back or a scheduled call back from a customer support agent to a specific end point or phone number. Another variation of this, customers can initiate a call directly to their Lync client from a contact center agent who also uses Lync 2013 for voice, instant messaging, and so on.

The use of federation in Lync is also helpful in customer care scenarios because through federation, voice, video, and metadata can be technically easy and economically transferred.

Contact center integration is a relatively complex topic because every project in this space comes with (or at least should have) a **Communication Enabled Business Process (CEBP)**. CEBP has to be analyzed and designed to achieve a cost efficient and logical communication process between customer and contact center agents.

In other words, every project opportunity is different and a deep understanding of the desired customer experience for communication and collaboration is required before a Lync integration can be designed and realized.

Common features and scenarios in contact center projects:

- Customer visits website and requests for support.
- Customer requests for a call back or schedules a call back on the web page.
- Customer is searching for information and chats with an automated IM bot to ask for help.
- Customer dials into a Lync-based support hotline/telephony queue and makes use of **Interactive Voice Response (IVR)** — options to be routed to a support agent.
- Customer uses a web chat interface to communicate with a support agent. Both sides use language translation to communicate to each other (for example, Spanish to English, English to Spanish, and so on).
- Customer can start a contextual web chat on Microsoft Lync to ask questions about a particular product/service by clicking on a link.
- Customer can convert the web chat into a voice call when they want to escalate their issue through the click of a button.
- Agent has all the data needed about the customer in a summary view to help them answer customer's questions about the product.
- Agent can escalate calls to any product expert who is available.
- The call center supervisor can track all calls and join in the calls when there are pressing issues that need their attention.

Although Lync 2013 offers many different ways to extend the base set of functionalities into the contact center space, another quick option is to select an available third-party solution created by a certified third-party software provider.

Microsoft offers an overview on all current *certified* and tested contact center software providers based on Lync 2010 and Lync 2013 technology. Companies like Clarity Connect, Aspect, Voxtron, PrairieFyre, Genesys, Zeacom, Luware, Interactive Intelligence, and many other providers do offer solutions for the contact center space and are ready to be integrated into the Lync customer environment. It is recommended to visit the Microsoft web page to read more about current development and available solutions in this space.

There are two types of contact centers; UC-enabled and UC-native. The first category works through plugins to pass the call from Lync through SIP trunking to another call control platform for processing. These call centers include Aspect, Interactive Intelligence, Geneys and Zeacom. The second utilizes Lync as a call control platform. Call centers that utilize this approach include Clarity Connect and PrarieFyer.

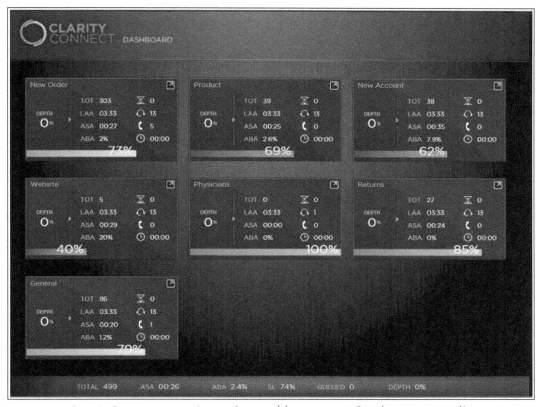

Lync in the contact center (source: `http://connect.claritycon.com/`)

Clarity Connect offers real-time reporting (dashboard) to extended communication features for contact center agents.

Skype and Lync

Skype plays a very important role along with Microsoft's Lync platform and other unified communications and collaboration market players. The Skype platform was first released in 2003 and was originally created by a very interesting group of developers (Janus Friis and Niklas Zennström) and a company known as KaZaA.

Microsoft's purchase of Skype in 2011 for around 8.5 billion USD was an important event for the real-time communication community. Microsoft is currently engaged in using Skype's backbone infrastructure and feature set for their customers.

Skype's rich feature set of instant messaging, video, and audio communication, as well as desktop sharing and VoIP, is used by more than 663 million registered end users around the globe. Skype allows users to have a voice chat via a simple microphone on the computer, video communication via a webcam, and text-based message chat via IM with any Skype user.

Skype is also integrated with the traditional telephony network (PSTN) to enable any calls out to a cell phone or fixed line phone around the world. Unlike most VoIP services, Skype is a hybrid peer-to-peer and client-server system. It makes use of background processing on computers running Skype software. Skype's original proposed name (Sky Peer-to-Peer) reflects this fact.

Since Skype merged with Microsoft, Lync comes closer to Skype from a technical perspective. Both platforms offer a rich collaboration and communication feature set where Lync is positioned as "Enterprise" solution for customers and Skype as the consumer, small, and medium business solution. In the cloud space, Microsoft's entry level of Office 365 cloud offering will also offer Skype for collaboration and communication for small and medium businesses.

We can expect the Skype and Lync platform to eventually merge at one point in the future to offer customers a single client experience in both the consumer and business space. Skype not only offers a rich feature set but also some very valuable add-ons for the Lync platform and an extensive backend infrastructure and VoIP implementation to telephone carriers around the world.

Merging Skype into Lync or combining these two platforms to create a new generation platform could create a huge competitive advantage against the current UC offerings. Customers could maximize the advantages of the VoIP telephony offering in both the consumer area and the enterprise business area to dramatically save telecommunication costs.

Although Lync and Skype are currently separate solutions for collaboration and communication, it is highly possible that the growth of Skype in consumer business and Lync in enterprise business would bring about very interesting and impactful innovations in the real-time communications space in the very near future.

Today, Lync 2013 and Skype are offering "federation" to each other for certain communication modalities. In other words, currently you are able to communicate by instant messaging and audio between Lync 2013 and Skype. The implementation is quite powerful for business because more than 300 million users are part of the worldwide Skype network in the consumer space. Lync allows communication to customers and business partners who are using Lync and also to other companies that are using Skype for business. This is a cost efficient and secure way to implement communication and collaboration. For example, Microsoft itself is using the Skype network as backbone to route voice traffic with much reduced cost through Microsoft support sites in the contact/customer care space and is also implementing Skype/Lync communication scenarios in specific spaces. Other companies and customers of Microsoft are using Skype/Lync as a "click to call" and "click to chat" solution on websites to engage customers with the right contact inside their own organization. Some other companies use Skype/Lync federation to allow their employees to be able to connect to private contacts in a well-managed way when they are away on business trips or on-site at projects.

Source: http://connect.claritycon.com/

Clarity Connect offers Skype and Lync integration/communication for customer care projects.

However, the current Skype/Lync federation is just the first step, with the further development of Skype and Lync we will see more communication modalities and major features coming together down the road and potentially much further improvements and innovations of both platforms in the roadmap. Let's stay tuned, we can only wait to see what the future offers.

Future development

Let us now take a look at the current trends and developments in the information and communications industry. We recognize that unified communications and Collaboration solutions will soon be a standard requirement in mid to large enterprise companies. In the past, IT and Telecommunications departments mostly operated independently and were jointly responsible for the acquisition and deployment of the most diverse technologies. Trends show that more and more companies combine their IT and Telecommunications departments when discussing about their telecommunications information technology solutions for the future.

The Internet, Web 2.0, and Web 3.0 solutions have also made web technologies an increasingly important aspect. The Internet has triggered many improvements and innovations in information and telecommunications over these past years and has also given birth to the term "social networking" and "real-time communication and collaboration" which have gained tremendous popularity. The term "social networks" refers to platforms which are on the Internet and via users, they can link to other users and virtually build the networking routes like meeting new people face to face before being officially introduced. Facebook is a good example where people build connection and relationships to other people by sharing information, content, contextual information such as current location or use it as a platform for selling and advertising products and services. These relationships are not only built for personal networking or simply just for hobbies, they can also help employees in companies with important business contacts to optimize their position in the value chain. Another benefit of social networking is the ability for users to organize themselves through their own network of relationships into discussion groups on technical or specific topics. Here again, real-time communication has played an important role in social networks, just like it did for the elements of unified communications and Collaboration. Social networking is increasingly used in the office environment and integrated into their daily work activity. In other words, enterprise social networks with large feature sets for communication and collaboration may be one of the megatrends in the next couple of years. To support this innovative development, many software and technology providers have also integrated these media into the office applications of tomorrow. Examples include Microsoft's acquisition of "Yammer", one of the potential future enterprise social networks in companies and Microsoft Suite 2013 (Office 2013) is now integrated with several hosted and available social networks. Cisco, IBM, and other major players in the technology market are also coming up with innovative solutions and platforms. An interesting example is Cisco's entry into this space with a product called "Cisco WebEx Social (Formerly Cisco Quad)", which contains elements of "Facebook" with real-time communication for the business environment.

For more information about Cisco WebEx Social go to
`http://www.cisco.com/web/products/quad/index.html`.

Another noticeable trend in the development and transformation of information and communication technology is in the direction of service-oriented providers. In short, new cloud service technologies have enabled the economical and optimized operation of various IT services such as e-mail, collaboration, software development, mobile solutions, virtualization, system management, UC, and many more. In this new field of technology, we use terms such as "on-premise", "online service", "cloud computing", and "cloud service", which will probably, in a few years, form a large part of today's IT and telecommunications infrastructure and also for collaboration solutions as a service. The term on-premise means that the software is stored in IT and data centers on-site and managed by the IT department locally. The term hybrid or cloud service means shifting them to external service providers. In short, this is a new, huge change in information technology and this is comparable to the introduction of the Internet. Companies and organizations will also have to adapt by changing to this new model. Security questions and other open questions such as regulatory systems will be resolved in time so software integration and operation will change tremendously. Microsoft, Google, IBM, Cisco, Apple, VMware, and many others are already developing, in addition to integration, tomorrow's solutions which are already increasingly being offered in an online and hosted solution scenario.

Some manufacturers already offer to customers the choice of, cloud service, on-premise, or hybrid implementation. Microsoft, for example offers the customers the choice to migrate completely into the cloud or continue to use a part of their own IT equipment. Almost every new Microsoft product is designed to integrate and operate in all three scenarios. This allows enterprises, for example, to have certain solutions to be partly integrated in their data center because of certain requirements, and outsource other parts onto Microsoft's cloud service.

Similarly, future versions of the unified communications and collaboration product, currently represented by the Lync Server 2013, Exchange Server 2013 (hosted integration only available together with Office 365 today), SharePoint Server 2013, Office 2013, and many other solutions will evolve based on the Microsoft Wave 16 strategy.

Another big megatrend is to bring "big data" into the cloud. Next to communication, collaboration, application, or social services, Gartner and other research institutes predict that from year 2011, the growth of data will be 48 percent in the next couple years and that 49 percent of CIO's data and **business intelligence (BI)** will be a very critical topic for their business.

The Megatrends the next years – from communication, collaboration to social, cloud, and data hosting (also BI)

For more information about upcoming megatrends go to `http://www.gartner.com/technology/home.jsp` or `http://www.forrester.com/home`, or `http://www.idc.com//home.jsp#.UVi8fmbn8dU`.

Another discernible trend toward cloud service is in the development platforms. Many applications and software solutions are designed for integration into data centers and IT departments of companies. Applications can be easily migrated when they are developed directly on the cost-effective and fail-safe cloud. One example is the Microsoft cloud service called Azure, where the developer can integrate applications into the cloud to reduce infrastructure costs and investment costs needed for their applications. Another example is that customers are able to run specific standard products of Microsoft in the Azure cloud. The idea here is the same, reducing the cost for the IT infrastructure plus allowing customization for the companies' own applications.

 For more information about Microsoft Azure: `http://www.windowsazure.com/en-us/pricing/free-trial/?WT.mc_id=azurebg_us_sem_branded_trialpage`.

The following diagram illustrates Microsoft Cloud Services example with Azure:

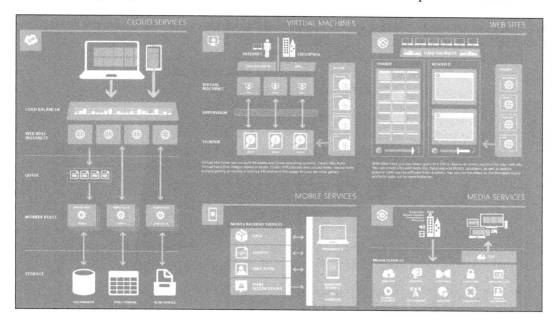

 The Microsoft Azure diagram is by Microsoft and can be downloaded at http://www.microsoft.com/en-us/download/details. aspx?id=35473.

Linked to this is the emergence of a new trend in mobile communication media. A few years ago, the development of mobile phones, have driven a steady innovation of novel technologies in different communication services, development of multifunctional mobile devices, smartphones, ultra-mobile PCs, portable pads, conference and communications equipment, and many other mobile technologies by companies such as Microsoft, Google, Cisco, Samsung, Dell, Sony, and many more. Since 2012, the trend from PC, Notebook to "Tablet PC" is one of the biggest markets for all hardware and software players. If the trend reports by Gartner, Forrester, IDC, and other research companies are right in visualizing our future, we will see a progressive merger of the different platforms such as Notebook, personal computer, the new generation of mobile devices, and other industry devices into touch-enabled tablet devices and they will be part of our daily social and business life. The current computer and device market is full of headlines and announcements of new technologies such as Apple iPad series, Microsoft Surface, Google Android, Amazon Kindle, BlackBerry, and many others. Some researchers believe that the era of PCs is at risk or over but perhaps it is more accurate to say that PCs are in the midst of a conversion; into something new and more mobile for businesses and consumers.

It is also a fact that few platforms can offer a high usability for both business use and private/consumer interest at the same time. This will change in the next couple of years but in today's tablet world, not every tablet can open a Microsoft Word, PowerPoint, or Excel document or enable users to access their business and private mailbox and calendar functions efficiently. Next to this, some areas such as consumer electronics and the gaming industry targets all platforms, including the PC and consoles for more sophisticated and complex use.

In addition to new features and areas, another long awaited industry development is the voice control operation by the Windows 8 touch technology, Windows Phone 8 series, Apple's iOS, Google's Android, and others. Based on the current view of today's technologies, there is a very specific focus to enable touch in devices and to simplify the user interface for the end users. This is one of the key competitive areas and is also related to all the new form factors of computers and devices. Speech, voice control, and natural language will be the future and will change the face of information technology further, a couple of years from now. The dream to communicate and use every device in a completely natural way will come true and our generation of users and business will be part of this future.

Closely related to this technological advancement is the integration of software into various objects such as room walls, touch pads, tables, glass walls, doors, and other innovations which will change our homes and offices of tomorrow. Speech technology with voice-based recognition, voice analytics and voice identification of people (users), and intelligent control are some of the major challenges for the information technology sector of tomorrow.

If you want to see some of the visions and innovations by current industry leaders such as, Microsoft, Google, and Cisco, check out the following links:

- Google Glass: http://www.google.com/glass/start/
- Cisco Future Visions: http://blogs.cisco.com/news/the-future-of-tv-coming-soon-to-a-wall-near-you/ or http://www.cisco.com/en/US/prod/collateral/ps10680/ps10683/ps10668/C11-657924_design_org_next_WP.pdf
- Microsoft Future Visions: http://www.microsoft.com/office/vision/ or http://techcrunch.com/2011/10/27/microsofts-vision-of-the-future-includes-touch-sensitive-everything-and-beautiful-people-only/

Future vision

In 10 to 20 years from now, will we use technology naturally at home and in businesses? Touch, Speech, and artificial intelligence will change the way we will live, work, play, and stay connected to others – Daniel Jonathan Valik.

[Read more on artificial intelligence at `http://en.wikipedia.org/wiki/Artificial_intelligence`.]

Summary

The extensive innovations described here will change many industries, regions, and even the way we work and think. Changes in these value chains, which are triggered by technological and sociological changes, have already begun. These changes are further accelerated by the new generation of knowledge workers/professionals and by the changes in global market economy such as booming energy technology, green innovations, and so on. How we work, where we work, and when we are efficient is redesigning the new work hours and workplace models. Even communication and collaboration across different time zones and hours will change with the availability of new technologies. We can only guess what possibilities and opportunities are associated with these changes.

Each generation has its own rate of development based on technology innovation and its challenges. We can only wait to see what our future generation will have, depending on our age and actions. It is clear that not all changes have positive effects, but change gives us the opportunity to create the world of tomorrow, so let us take the first steps into a new generation of communication and collaboration for your business.

OPERATING AGREEMENT[1]

For the use and operation of IP-based Real-time communication solutions

Between

Contoso Ltd

and

Contoso Employee Association, represented by the president Daniel Jonathan Valik, according to the following agreement:

PREAMBLE

There is an agreement between the management of Contoso and the Contoso Employee Association on the use of modern communication solutions needed in the company to increase the competitiveness of the company. The resulting requirements for their use may be in the interest of the company and the employees.

The purpose of this Operating Agreement is to develop business advantage through the use of advanced communication solutions and also to safeguard the privacy of the employees, especially in their rights to protect personal data and not be monitored for performance.

1. Scope
    a. The operating agreement governs objectively the operation and use of IP-based real-time communication solutions (such as Lync Server, Lync Online, etc.) offering communication functions, such as telephony and Enterprise Voice, conferencing, file transfer, application sharing and instant messaging.
    b. This Operating Agreement covers everything except specific operating agreements containing provisions that are inconsistent with those listed and is covered in under the special operating agreement.

c. The geographical scope extends to all operations of the Employer, as well as home offices.

d. The personal scope extends to all workers employed by the employer under the Federal Data Protection Act § 5 paragraph 1 and apply mutatis mutandis to the personal data of former employees.

2. The Purpose

The purpose of this Operating Agreement is to develop business advantage through the use of advanced communication solutions and also to safeguard the privacy rights of the employees, especially in their rights to protect personal data and not be monitored for performance.

Through greater use of audio and video conferencing, by reducing email volume and elimination of dedicated telephone systems brings about business advantages inter alia a more direct and efficient communication, for example, in the form of reduction in the number of business travels.

Currently classic telephony inter alia Microsoft Lync Server, Lync Online and Exchange Unified Messaging are used for real-time communications, audio and video conferences / presentations and training in the company.

3. Functional Areas

i. Presence

The Presence function provides information about the communication partner (For example: communication and organizational data) and his/her presence information: whether online, absent, active on the PC, in a meeting, etc.

These usage data may not be used in any way to monitor the interactions and conduct of employees/colleagues.

The "Tag" function which provides information about status change and presence information for employees / colleagues may not be used in any way to determine the productivity of the employee. No employee is required to be included in any contact lists. Each employee can decide who they share their presence information with and can choose to change their status at any time or even turn it off completely.

No logging of presence information is allowed (For example server side logging or custom application for presence based statistics.).

ii. Instant Messaging (IM)

Instant messaging enables the exchange of text in real time. There can be two or more employees engaged in an IM session. Similarly, the exchange of texts with users of other systems (such as AOL, MSN/Live Messenger, Skype and other services using PIC - Public IM Connectivity) or with employees of other companies (by Federation) is possible.

Content of the communication may be recorded:

   a. Central record of the content of the communication is permitted only if this is made possible by the Federal Data Protection Act (§ 3 paragraph 1). Call data is logged only if this is explicitly required by law.

   b. Local recording / storage may take place only if

       All Communication partners give their consent

       All employees have to follow the regulations set by the Company accordingly

       Records shall not be used for power or in the monitoring of staff performance

iii. Audio and Video Communication (Conferencing)

Employees can communicate with each other through the means of audio and video communication (For Example: via Lync online meetings). Since Live images via web cam can be transmitted and individual employee can decide whether he or she allows it. Audio and video content can be recorded locally by the organizers on the hard disk after prior consent of all participants in the conference. Recordings of the conference may be used as meeting minutes and for future training purposes.

Content of the communication may be recorded:

   a. Central record of the content of the communication is permitted only if this is made possible by the Federal Data Protection Act (§ 3 paragraph 1). Connection data is recorded only if this is required by law explicitly.

   b. Local recording / storage may take place only if all communication partners give their consent. Recordings may not be used to judge an employee's communication abilities, work efficiency and use it as a basis for their performance review.

Unless all parties agree, any record is deleted after three months. This does not apply to records of presentations, lectures and training courses which are carried out without active involvement of the participants in the communication.

Records shall not be used for performance or behavioral surveillance of employees

iv. Telephony

The use of technology allows phone calls from personal computers and IP phones (For example Polycom or Jabra devices)

- To other workstations inside and outside the company
- To internal telephones
- To internal IP phones
- To the public telephone network

Contents of such calls will not be recorded or logged. Call data is logged only if it is explicitly required by law. (See Federal Data Protection Act, § 3 paragraph 1)

4. External Conferencing Service

About the Lync Online (meeting) service provided on the Internet: All employees can initiate Audio and / or video conferences with internal and external people.

The employer is responsible for ensuring that the Lync Online communication and collaboration service provider is in compliance with all the rules and regulations of this agreement.

5. Data / Interface

There are no processing method interfaces to personal data except for billing purposes and for ensuring technical operability (See Federal Data Protection Act, § 3 paragraph 1)

6. Evaluations

No personal evaluations must be created except for billing purposes and to ensure the technical operability (See Federal Data Protection Act, § 3 paragraph

7. Performance or Behavioral Surveillance

   Monitoring of performance or behavior of employees cannot be done for the purpose of individual assessment and must be in accordance to § 87 paragraph 1 item 6 of the Federal Data Protection Act. Any information obtained in violation of this Operating Agreement shall be ineffective.

8. Privacy/Information Security

   Privacy must be respected in accordance with statutory and company regulations.

   The legal department of the organization or a dedicated privacy and compliance team (external resources or internal of the company) will act as the Privacy officer.

   Before automated processing, modification or extension of personal data, the corresponding message must be first handed over to a competent data protection officer.

   Operational rules for information security must be observed. The officer acts as the liaison for information security in an advisory capacity.

9. Rights of the Works

   Contoso Employee Association has the legal rights to access any data and reports made by this technology.

   Contoso Employee Association will inform all users and obtain consent from users for all intended changes, especially in the release of new features in the area of real-time communications (Such as Microsoft Lync Server and Lync Online services/Office 365).

   If there is a dispute in how real-time communication is implemented and used based on this non-operating agreement, the Employee Association or the Employee have to resolve this in accordance to the Federal Data Protection Act § 76 paragraph 5.

10. Final Provisions

    a. This Agreement shall be enforced upon signature.

    b. The operating agreement may be terminated with a notice period of 6 months, but not before the xx.yy.zzzz. Upon termination, its regulations shall immediately enter negotiations with the management and the Contoso Employee Association over its continuation and adaptation of this Operating Agreement.

    c. When regulations of this agreement are deemed invalid or inappropriate, you may replace them with more relevant rules. Individual rules can be changed, repealed or amended at any time by mutual consent.

Reference:

1. Laws are based on the EU Federal Data Act which can be found on:
   `http://www.gesetze-im-internet.de/englisch_bdsg/index.html`

Index

overall concept 126-128
role 111, 112
selecting 143, 144
training implementation 126
unified communications. *See* UC
Unified Communications Managed API
    (UCMA) 80, 118
Unified Communications platform
  advantages 77-79
Unified Communications Web App
    (UCWA) 79, 118, 138
Unified Presence solution 47
Universal Mobile Telecommunications
    Systems (UMTS) 92
University of California
  URL 31
User Acceptance Testing (UAT) 124, 149
US National Science Foundation 10

V

Verizon 20, 52
video conferencing technologies 53
virtualization 169
virtual LAN (VLAN) 172
Virtual Private Network (VPN) 95
voicemail 12, 15

Voice over Internet Protocol (VoIP) 16, 70
VSee
  about 118
  URL 119

W

Web 2.0 26
Web-based Real Time Communication. *See*
    Web RTC
Web RTC
  URL 86, 114
Wi-Fi 12
Wikipedia
  URL 38
workflows 29
World Wide Web 11

X

XING 17, 114

Y

Yahoo Messenger 36
YouTube
  about 34
  as video knowledge portal 34-38

Thank you for buying
Microsoft Lync 2013 Unified Communications: From
Telephony to Real-time Communication in the Digital Age

About Packt Publishing

Packt, pronounced 'packed', published its first book "Mastering phpMyAdmin for Effective MySQL Management" in April 2004 and subsequently continued to specialize in publishing highly focused books on specific technologies and solutions.

Our books and publications share the experiences of your fellow IT professionals in adapting and customizing today's systems, applications, and frameworks. Our solution based books give you the knowledge and power to customize the software and technologies you're using to get the job done. Packt books are more specific and less general than the IT books you have seen in the past. Our unique business model allows us to bring you more focused information, giving you more of what you need to know, and less of what you don't.

Packt is a modern, yet unique publishing company, which focuses on producing quality, cutting-edge books for communities of developers, administrators, and newbies alike. For more information, please visit our website: www.packtpub.com.

About Packt Enterprise

In 2010, Packt launched two new brands, Packt Enterprise and Packt Open Source, in order to continue its focus on specialization. This book is part of the Packt Enterprise brand, home to books published on enterprise software – software created by major vendors, including (but not limited to) IBM, Microsoft and Oracle, often for use in other corporations. Its titles will offer information relevant to a range of users of this software, including administrators, developers, architects, and end users.

Writing for Packt

We welcome all inquiries from people who are interested in authoring. Book proposals should be sent to author@packtpub.com. If your book idea is still at an early stage and you would like to discuss it first before writing a formal book proposal, contact us; one of our commissioning editors will get in touch with you.

We're not just looking for published authors; if you have strong technical skills but no writing experience, our experienced editors can help you develop a writing career, or simply get some additional reward for your expertise.

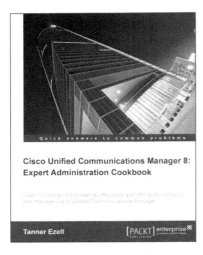

Cisco Unified Communications Manager 8:
Expert Administration Cookbook

Tanner Ezell   [PACKT] enterprise 88

Cisco Unified Communications Manager 8: Expert Administration Cookbook

ISBN: 978-1-84968-432-3   Paperback: 310 pages

Over 110 advanced recipes to effectively and efficiently configure and manage Cisco Unified Communications Manager

1. Full of illustrations, diagrams, and tips with clear step-by-step instructions and real time examples

2. Master call admission control and the technologies associated with it, which is an important aspect of any unified communications deployment to ensure call quality and resilience

FreeSWITCH
Cookbook

Over 40 recipes to help you get the most out of your
FreeSWITCH server

Anthony Minessale   Darren Schreiber   [   ] open source
Michael S Collins   Raymond Chandler

FreeSWITCH Cookbook

ISBN: 978-1-84951-540-5   Paperback: 150 pages

Over 40 recipes to help you get the most out of your FreeSWITCH server

1. Get powerful FreeSWITCH features to work for you

2. Route calls and handle call detailing records

3. Written by members of the FreeSWITCH development team

Building Telephony Systems with OpenSIPS 1.6

ISBN: 978-1-84951-074-5   Paperback: 284 pages

Build scalable and robust telephony systems using SIP

1. Build a VoIP Provider based on the SIP Protocol

2. Cater to scores of subscribers efficiently with a robust telephony system based in pure SIP

3. Gain a competitive edge using the most scalable VoIP technology

4. Learn how to avoid pitfalls using precise billing

5. Packed with rich practical examples and case studies on the latest OpenSIPS version 1.6

WCF 4.0 Multi-tier Services Development with LINQ to Entities

ISBN: 978-1-84968-114-8   Paperback: 348 pages

Build SOA applications on the Microsoft platform with this hands-on guide updated for VS2010

1. Master WCF and LINQ to Entities concepts by completing practical examples and applying them to your real-world assignments

2. The first and only book to combine WCF and LINQ to Entities in a multi-tier real-world WCF service

3. Ideal for beginners who want to build scalable, powerful, easy-to-maintain WCF services

Please check **www.PacktPub.com** for information on our titles

www.ingramcontent.com/pod-product-compliance
Lightning Source LLC
LaVergne TN
LVHW062314060326
832902LV00013B/2215